JUBILEE OF HOPE

Archbishop Rino Fisichella

Translated by Ronnie Convery

Our Sunday Visitor
Huntington, Indiana

29 28 27 26 25 24 1 2 3 4 5 6 7 8 9

Our Sunday Visitor Publishing Division
Our Sunday Visitor, Inc.
200 Noll Plaza
Huntington, IN 46750
1-800-348-2440

ISBN: 978-1-63966-323-1 (Inventory No. T2884)
eISBN: 978-1-63966-324-8
LCCN: 2024949167

Cover design: Tyler Ottinger
Cover art: Alamy
Interior design: Amanda Falk

PRINTED IN THE UNITED STATES OF AMERICA

Table of Contents

Introduction

A Jubilee with a difference

Spes non confundit ("Hope does not disappoint"). With this expression [and the title of Pope Francis' bull of indiction announcing a Holy Year], both simple yet so full of meaning, we are preparing to celebrate the Ordinary Jubilee of 2025. It will be a Jubilee bathed in the light of hope. We are not used to a "thematic" Holy Year. It is true that if you look back over recent jubilees you can find some underlying theme, but it has never been quite as explicit as in this case. Pope Pius XII wanted the 1950 Jubilee to be celebrated in the context of the reconstruction after the Second World War; in 1975, Pope Paul VI insisted on the theme of unity, ten years after the conclusion of the Second Vatican Council, a period which saw the Church living through a period of conflict and tension. The Jubilee of 2000 was inevitably Christological, marking as it did, the close of the second millennium of our history.

The Extraordinary Jubilee of 2015 was an exception, because Pope Francis very explicitly wanted it to be marked as a Holy Year entirely dedicated to the theme of mercy. In his vespers homily on March 13, 2015, taking everyone by surprise, he made an announcement no one expected: "I have often thought about how the Church can make her mission of being a witness to mercy more evident. It is a journey that begins with a spiritual conversion; and we must make this journey. This is why I have decided to announce an *Extraordinary Jubilee* that has God's mercy at its center. It will be a *Holy Year of Mercy*. We want to live it in the light of the word of the Lord: 'Be merciful as the Father is merciful.'"

That Jubilee was extraordinary in every sense. It was celebrated in each local church in a surprising way; "Doors of Mercy" were opened in every cathedral, in shrines, and even in hospitals. The pope showed the way, when — breaking with tradition — he opened a Door of Mercy a few weeks early, November 29, in the Cathedral of Bangui in the Central African Republic, a land riven by internal conflicts, his aim being to offer a concrete sign that this Jubilee was to be literally "extraordinary."

I remember the phone call Pope Francis made to me a few weeks before leaving for that apostolic journey, asking me what I thought about it. "Holy Father," I said, "it will be a wonderful sign, especially for a country which is suffering as much as that land."

"You know," the pope replied, "the nuncio suggested it to me …"

"I totally agree," I said, "and it will be a sign that I don't think will obscure in any way the opening of the Holy Door in St. Peter's. Indeed, it will give that ceremony even more meaning."

That Jubilee Year really was extraordinary. The expression that so many bishops used when talking to me about it was: "I have never seen so many people …"

This Jubilee of 2025, however, is part of the ordinariness of history. It will be the twenty-seventh since the first "ordinary" Holy Year called by Pope Boniface VIII in 1300. Despite this, or perhaps precisely *because* of this, it will be marked as the first

Jubilee of the 21st century and will bear all the hallmarks of the innovations we are now living with in daily life. First, a new culture is changing our lives in a powerful way, yet there is an almost total lack of awareness of this taking place. We are living through the birth of a new culture that no one foresaw. Those who are used to making comparisons with the past will find that this Jubilee does not have much in common with the Holy Year St. John Paul II celebrated in 2000.

The 2000 Jubilee was in the mind of that holy pope from the very beginning of his pontificate. His first encyclical, *Redemptor Hominis*, bears witness to this. Indeed, right at the start we read these words:

> The Redeemer of man, Jesus Christ, is the center of the universe and of history. To him go my thoughts and my heart in this solemn moment of the world that the Church and the whole family of present-day humanity are now living. In fact, this time, in which God in his hidden design has entrusted to me, after my beloved predecessor John Paul I, the universal service of the Chair of Saint Peter in Rome, is already very close to the year 2000. At this moment it is difficult to say what mark that year will leave on the face of human history or what it will bring to each people, nation, country, and continent, in spite of the efforts already being made to foresee some events. For the Church, the People of God spread, although unevenly, to the most distant ends of the earth, it will be the year of a great Jubilee. We are already approaching that date, which, without prejudice to all the corrections imposed by chronological exactitude, will recall and reawaken in us in a special way our awareness of the key truth of faith which Saint John expressed at the beginning of his Gospel: "The Word became flesh

> and dwelt among us." (1)

That Holy Year of 2000 took place in a very particular context. The pope was already ill, but he was still strong and determined to carry forward the objective of his pontificate. He used a stick, but how he liked to play with it, twirling it around to bring smiles to the millions of young people who had flocked to Tor Vergata in Rome. After a challenging speech in which he invited young people to create a "faith laboratory," he improvised, adding some lighthearted remarks:

> There is a Polish proverb that says: "*Kto z kim przestaje, takim si? Staje.*" That means that if you live with young people, you become young, too! So, I will return home rejuvenated. … I greet all of you once more, especially those who are further back, in the shadows, who can't see anything. But even if they can't see, they can certainly hear this noisy racket. This 'racket' has hit Rome and Rome will never forget it!

Those words of his remain as the core message of that speech in which he called everyone to be "watchmen of the morning."

The most high-tech thing we had available to us for that Jubilee was email. There was no internet as we know it today: there was no Facebook, much less TikTok or *Instagram*; there was only email, which was fascinating in its own way, but printed paper was still in widespread use. WhatsApp hadn't even entered the mind of its inventor, and "traditional" forms of communication were still very much in use. Today, this is no longer the case. The digital culture reigns supreme and it is impossible to ignore it. Today, the mobile phone is no longer a tool, but a part of ourselves that we can barely live without.

In the era of the *metaverse*, we should be able to communicate in an even more direct way, but in the Church we cannot always keep pace with what the world is experiencing. Here there are still too many delays and only slowly — too slowly — are we becoming aware that we are faced with a new culture which, unlike the past, is truly globalized and radically changes our way of living and thinking.

Young people who are now twenty-five don't even know what the Jubilee of 2000 was. Their parents and perhaps their grandparents know. But these young people need to understand and be taught about an event that only occurs every twenty-five years. And to do that we have to use their way of communicating, their language, their culture. It's not a mystery to anyone anymore. Those who are twenty-five years old quite simply no longer understand what we say. Our homilies and catecheses leave them completely indifferent, not because of the content we transmit, but because of the language we use, which is no longer *their* language and, therefore, has no impact on them. It doesn't communicate effectively with them. Religious ignorance thus increases and, with it, indifference toward those ideas which could help them engage with the spiritual and transcendent dimension of life.

Thinking about a Jubilee in the internet age, therefore, requires making choices that will have an impact on this new culture and reach people's minds and hearts. Some priests have grasped this well and are able to communicate well. The majority of our formators, bishops, priests, teachers, and catechists though are not yet fully aware of the epochal transition we are living through. Here it is not just about using the cell phone, but of understanding that we are faced with a genuine anthropological turning point. The new digital culture is directly affecting the formation and vision of a new model of humanity, where the fundamental values that have been held for centuries are now plunged into crisis.

First and foremost, the themes of truth and freedom. To pretend this is not happening, or to ignore this momentous change, is equivalent to not accepting our responsibility for the evangelizing mission which engages the Church in every era, and in every time and culture. It is a matter of urgency, therefore, that we find people who are not only capable of communicating, but of being "watchmen of the morning" when faced with an epochal challenge like the one we are now experiencing.

We know that we are entering an arena where the giants dominate, especially at an economic level (something which is obvious but hidden). Yet, we are called upon to be "experts in humanity," as Saint Paul VI liked to say, and we must be aware that the challenge, although unequal, has to be accepted and faced for the good of humanity. We are all called to this task, and for us believers it would be an act of cowardly laziness not to be up for the challenge.

On the other hand, the theme chosen for the celebration of this Jubilee, hope, imposes on us a certain evangelical realism often eclipsed by an insistence on other issues which, although important, no longer attract people. I believe that today there is a great need for hope. It is something we hear every day because the global context causes people to experience fear, anxiety, and generalized uncertainty — something that affects young people personally. This can lead to feelings of desperation if young people are not properly supported. They need to hear a message that restores the certainty of true hope.

Pope Francis sums it up perfectly when he writes:

> The Christian community should be at the forefront in pointing out the need for a social covenant to support and foster hope, one that is inclusive and not ideological, working for a future filled with the laughter of babies and children, in order to fill the empty cradles in so many parts of our world. All of us, however, need to re-

> cover the joy of living, since men and women, created in the image and likeness of God (cf. Gn 1:26), cannot rest content with getting along one day at a time, settling for the "here and now" and seeking fulfillment in material realities alone. This leads to a narrow individualism and the loss of hope; it gives rise to a sadness that lodges in the heart and brings forth fruits of discontent and intolerance. (*Spes Non Confundit*, 9)

One final consideration is needed in light of the following reference made in *Spes non confundit*: "The Holy Year will also guide our steps towards yet another fundamental celebration for all Christians: 2033 will mark the two thousandth anniversary of the redemption won by the passion, death and resurrection of the Lord Jesus" (6). In some ways, this Holy Year becomes a preparation for what is to come in a few years' time, when we will celebrate the two thousandth anniversary of the death of Jesus. Just as in the year 2000, when the Church commemorated the mystery of the Incarnation of the Son of God, so in 2033 we will celebrate with great intensity the mystery of the death and resurrection of Jesus Christ — the event that changed the history of humanity. In that death, the love of God is truly revealed.

On Golgotha, Jesus reveals to us that God loves us to the point of giving all of himself. On the cross it becomes clear not only that God loves us, but also *how* he loves us. And the mystery of love reaches its culmination after three days, when the Risen One appears to his disciples and proclaims victory over death. The hope which lies at the core of the next Jubilee, therefore, becomes the fundamental and necessary premise for approaching the mystery of the Redemption in all its significance. Pope Francis wrote: "Hope is born from love and is founded on love" (*Spes Non Confundit*, 3). That's exactly it! That expression is like an antiphon that introduces us to the Jubilee of the Redemption and helps us to discover the richness of the Trinitarian love of God that never ceases to flow from the open side of the Crucified Christ, offering a love that knows no interruption and no limit.

So, we can see an impressive continuity between the celebration of one Jubilee and preparations for the next. The history of the Church thrives on this continuity — a continuity of the coherent transmission of the content of faith which spans centuries, from one generation to the next. The Jubilee falls within this context and offers the holy people of God the opportunity to be direct participants and living instruments of evangelization.

The following pages will try to explore the novelty of the 2025 Jubilee through its specific signs, which, when properly understood, will help us to live the Jubilee experience more knowingly and, I hope, more spiritually. The history of many centuries of Jubilees has seen an increase in signs and symbols which have gradually become part of the heritage of an event that still fascinates us today through its various rites and the message it offers. These signs will help us to revive the hope that every person experiences, deep in their hearts, a desire for a true and meaningful future.

The meaning of the Holy Year

Each Jubilee is celebrated for its own particular reason. We should not dismiss the idea that, in the plan of salvation which governs our personal actions and community events, the Lord sets aside certain moments of grace that he uses to support the path of the Church through time.

If the reason for each Jubilee were to be summed up in just one idea, however, it would surely be that of effectively announcing the grace of forgiveness and mercy. That is a difficult task in the modern world, so often marked by violence and the inability of people to forgive. In fact, it is precisely in this word, *forgiveness*, that the novelty of the Jubilee is summed up. It is a term that embodies the essence of the revelation of Jesus Christ who came so that we could be reconciled with the Father (cf. Eph 2:14–18).

A glance over the history of religions shows with certain clarity that where there is a manifestation of the sacred there is often associated with it a set-aside space and time which in some way evokes the transcendent for everyone.

The history of Israel, despite its peculiarities, exemplifies this idea. The tent in the desert and the Temple in Jerusalem are both signs of Yahweh's presence among his people. Even in the realm of time, sacredness was expressed through the celebration of festivals and feasts which had the primary purpose of keeping the memory of the events of salvation alive. The God who "with a strong hand and a powerful arm" had freed his people, leading them to the promised land, was regularly remembered through liturgical feasts. The feasts of tabernacles, of unleavened bread and of weeks (Shavuot), to name just a few of the best-known examples, had the aim of helping the people not to forget. Oblivion, which is the enemy of memory, was avoided through the celebration of feasts and festivals that occurred regularly at a specified time.

The jubilee year of the Old Testament fit into this context. It was calculated, in all likelihood, using a weekly cycle, which was a fundamental starting point for considering the sacred value of time in Israel. According to divine law, at the end of seven weeks of years [seven multiplied by seven] a year was set aside for the celebration of liberation:

> You shall count seven Sabbaths of years for yourselves, seven times seven years, and your span of seven times seven years will be forty-nine years. You shall blow the trumpet of the Jubilee on the tenth day of the seventh month, on the Day of Atonement you shall blow the trumpet throughout the land. You shall consecrate the fiftieth year, and proclaim liberty throughout the whole land to all of its inhabitants. It will be a Jubilee for you.

> Each of you shall return to his own property, and each shall return to his own clan. The fiftieth year shall be a Jubilee for you. You shall not sow nor reap. You shall not reap what grows on its own, and you shall not gather grapes from the undressed vines. It is a Jubilee and it is to be holy for you. You shall eat only what comes directly from the fields. In the Jubilee Year you shall return each man to his property. (Leviticus 25:8–13; cf. Exodus 21:2; 23:10; Deuteronomy 15:1)

The underlying significance of this can be understood in the context of sacred history. Every action of man, and even of the earth, must be seen in the light of God's action. Just as the Lord rested on the seventh day, so the earth, livestock, all creation, and man himself must rest; this allows the contemplation of God's creative action.

It is not clear whether the people of Israel ever celebrated a jubilee precisely as commanded in the Book of Leviticus. What is clear, however, is that the history of Christian Jubilees finds a solid foundation in the fourth chapter of the Gospel of Luke. This beautiful section of the Gospel is well-known. After the first successes of his preaching, Jesus returns to his hometown of Nazareth and as was his custom, on the Sabbath he went to the synagogue. Here, opening the scroll of the Book of Isaiah, he comments on the words of the prophet: "The Spirit of the Lord is upon me, / because he has anointed me / to bring the good news to the poor. / He has sent me to proclaim release to prisoners / and recovery of sight to the blind, / to let the oppressed go free, / and to proclaim the year of the Lord's favor" (Lk 4:18–19).

The year of mercy that Jesus announces is the basis of every Christian Jubilee and gives it its deepest meaning.

1
The Jubilee of Hope

"Hope in the LORD! Stand firm, / take heart and hope in the LORD!" (Ps 27:14). This verse of Psalm 27 is placed by Pope Francis at the conclusion of his letter announcing the Jubilee year. This is surely no coincidence. The final words of the bull are an invitation to never let oneself be deprived of hope when faced with any problem or difficulty in life. It is an invitation to be strong in a faith that supports hope, together with charity, and, therefore, to pursue a lifestyle based on the theological virtues, presenting this as a coherent form of Christian life.

A quick look at the psalm allows us to immediately grasp the underlying meaning, and it emerges that the sacred author intends to retrace the same themes as those contained in the more famous Psalm 23: "The LORD is my shepherd." In our psalm we are faced with an invocation addressed to God, who is our "light and salvation" and the "defense of my life," to thank him for the security he offers to those facing difficulties. "When evildoers close in on me / to devour my flesh, / it is they, my adversaries and enemies, / who stumble and fall. / Even if an army encamps against me, / my heart will not succumb to fear; / even if war breaks out against me, / I will not have my trust shaken" (Ps 27:2–3).

The description of the difficulties becomes even more dramatic when we get into the specifics: "Even if my father and mother abandon me, / the LORD will gather me up / Do not abandon me to the will of my adversaries, / for lying witnesses have risen against / breathing forth violence" (vv. 10, 12). The psalmist's conviction in describing this situation becomes a prelude to his asking God to offer the guarantee of his presence: "You who have been my help. / Do not reject or forsake me / O God, my savior" (v. 9). Thus the conclusion of the psalm becomes a synthesis of the entire plea, taking the form of an appeal to hope in God, who is invoked as the sole and ultimate meaning of life.

We find the same appeal in Psalm 42, which is written along similar lines, retracing the same theme — namely, the desire to reach God: "As a deer longs for streams of water, / so my soul longs for you, O God. / My soul thirsts for God, for the living God" (vv. 2–3). But the psalmist is hindered by the difficulties of life: "My tears have become my food / day and night / My soul is disheartened within me" (vv. 4, 7). For this reason, the believer turns with trust to God, certain of his saving intervention: "Place you hope in God, / for I will once again praise him, / my savior and my God" (v. 6). Once again, the believer sees hope as the content of a faith which does not disappoint.

The certainty of hope

This call to hope at the conclusion of the bull reminds us of the beginning of the pope's letter where the quote from the apostle Paul is stated quite clearly: "Hope does not disappoint." In fact, the entire reflection Pope Francis offers us revolves around this theme of the *certainty* of Christian hope. Step by step we are led into the great mystery of Christian hope, which is often more something we experience than something we reflect upon. Yet we, who are so used to rationalizing everything that we forget those things which are essential, often focus on reason alone and require the help of other, more coherent forms of knowledge to grasp their meaning. Defining hope (in the sense of wanting to express a rationally defined concept) seems not only difficult, but ultimately impossible. Our linguistic tool kit lacks the means necessary to contain a concept such as hope in a "linguistic cage." The definition escapes us, because life cannot be confined within a space limited by the primacy of reason alone.

So how can we have certainty about hope if it is a reality which, by its nature, concerns the future and which is — by definition — never fully knowable? Pope Francis briefly addresses this when he writes:

Christian hope does not deceive or disappoint because it is grounded in the certainty that nothing and no one may ever separate us from God's love:

> "Who then can separate us from the love of Christ? Will hardship, or distress, or persecution, or famine, or nakedness, or danger, or the sword? No, throughout all these things we are conquerors because of him who loved us. For I am convinced that neither death, nor life, nor angels, nor principalities, nor present things, nor things to come, nor powers, nor height, nor depth, nor any other creature will be able to separate us from the love of God in Christ Jesus our Lord" (Rom 8:35, 37–39).
>
> Here we see the reason why this hope perseveres in the midst of trials: founded on faith and nurtured by charity, it enables us to press forward in life. (*Spes Non Confundit*, 3)

The citing of this famous text from the Letter to the Romans allows us to take a step toward explaining the certainty of Christian hope. Perhaps in no other text of the New Testament do we find such a deep and firm conviction as that which is contained in these verses. Paul writes a veritable hymn about his unshakable certainty in God's love. The entire eighth chapter is dedicated to hope. The apostle, in his correspondence with the Christians of Rome, states determinedly that the reason for their hope is the liberation from sin and death brought about by Christ. The beginning of the chapter sets it our clearly: "Hence, there is now no condemnation for those who are in Christ Jesus. For the law of the Spirit of life in Christ Jesus has set you free from the law of sin and death" (vv. 1–2).

Christians have thus received a new life through baptism and live in the presence of the Holy Spirit which makes us "heirs of Christ" and prompts us to look forward to our own resurrection:

> You, however, do not live according to the flesh but according to the Spirit, since the Spirit of God dwells in you. Anyone who does not possess the Spirit of Christ cannot belong to him. But if Christ is in you, then even though the body is dead as a result of sin, the Spirit is alive in you because of righteousness. If the Spirit of him who raised Jesus from the dead dwells in you, then the one who raised Christ from the dead will also give life to your mortal bodies through his Spirit that dwells in you. (Romans 8:9–11)

Life in the Spirit, therefore, already allows us to possess the "first fruits of the Spirit," to truly be "children of God" and to await definitive salvation because "in hope we are saved" (Rom 8:24). Reading these phrases, it is easy to understand the apostle's sense of wonder and amazement — emotions which are expressed rhetorically in the question: "What then can we say in response to all this?" (v. 31). Nothing and no one will ever be able to separate a believer in Christ from Christ's love for him. Paul is not only certain of this, but he is persuaded, indeed "convinced" (v. 38) of it. The Greek expression used by the apostle (*pèpeismai*) confirms his absolute, rocklike trust in the love of God. This love, therefore, is the origin, source, and foundation of the certainty which constitutes his hope in salvation. There is no alternative to this, because it is the result of the presence of the Holy Spirit who acts in such a way as to make certain the outpouring of God's love on those who believe in him. We thus return to the initial statement that permeates the whole papal bull: "Hope does not disappoint, because the love of God has been poured into our hearts through the Holy Spirit who has been given to us" (cf. Rom 5:5). Surrendering oneself to the love of God, with trust, therefore, is at the origin of the hope that exists in every baptized person giving them the certainty of salvation.

As can be seen, the certainty of hope that derives from love forces us to abandon all individualism and self-sufficiency to become more aware of the primacy of grace that acts upon and justifies the sinner, obtaining salvation for him. This is the context in which the theme of "justification" arises; it is an essential theme if we are to fully understand the teaching on hope. The apostle, expounding his teaching on hope, states that in Jesus Christ — and through our faith in him — God has justified us:

> At the appointed time, while we were still helpless, Christ died for the ungodly. Indeed, it is seldom that anyone will die for a just person, although perhaps for a good person someone might be willing to die. Thus, God proved his love for us in that while we were still sinners Christ died for us. And so, now that we have been justified by Christ's blood, how much more certainly will

> we be saved through him from divine retribution. For if, while we were enemies, we were reconciled to God through the death of his Son, how much more certain it is that, having been reconciled, we shall be saved by his life. (Romans 5:6–10)

In this text we encounter an intriguing and, in some ways, very difficult word to translate into modern languages — namely, *justification*. It is as if Paul wanted to say that on the cross, in that unique act of love with which God himself reveals *how* he loves, his "anger" for the sins of men was destroyed. What we might call the wrath of God is destroyed. This is a theme that often appears in Sacred Scripture but finds little space in modern reflections because it seems to us to be absurd: How can a God who is love show wrath or anger?

The apostle's teaching, however, is very encouraging: God's wrath in a sense crashes against the cross on which Jesus hangs and is destroyed there. Henceforth the Law is superseded, because believers are made partakers of the new life of baptism that introduces them to the faith of the Church. The justification that occurred in the past, through which we obtained peace with God (cf. Rom 5:1), now allows us to live in grace. All of us, therefore, can boast of the gift received: We have abandoned sin and live anchored to grace. This is not only the way the Father justifies us by reconciling us with himself, but also constitutes the reality of ordinary life for every Christian. In short, if we turn our gaze to the past, we see that we have been justified. If we look to the present, we can see firsthand that we live under the primacy of grace. And when our gaze turns to the future, then the real strength of hope emerges.

Having the certainty of hope, therefore, means being convinced of God's love for us: He will never abandon us. To reassure us on this point, the apostle recalls the figure of Abraham:

"Though he hoped against hope, he believed" (Rom 4:18). Just as Abraham was certain — based on the word of the Lord — that he would become "the father of many nations" (also 4:18), so every believer can be strong in hope, having the certainty that he shares the very life of God and that in the future he will also enjoy his glory (cf. Rom 5:2).

The patience of waiting

Of course, the future to which hope refers also requires *waiting* as a prerequisite The theme of waiting leads us into another theme which is closely connected to it — namely, that of *patience*. There is an interesting reference to patience in the papal bull when it states that it is "a virtue closely related to hope":

> In our fast-paced world, we are used to wanting everything now. We no longer have time simply to be with others; even families find it hard to get together and enjoy one another's company. Patience has been put to flight by frenetic haste, and this has proved detrimental, since it leads to impatience, anxiety, and even gratuitous violence, resulting in more unhappiness and self-centeredness.
>
> Nor is there much place for patience in this age of the internet, as space and time yield to an ever-present "now." Were we still able to contemplate creation with a sense of awe, we might better understand the importance of patience. We could appreciate the changes of the seasons and their harvests, observe the life of animals and their cycles of growth, and enjoy the clarity of vision of Saint Francis. In his *Canticle of the Creatures*, written exactly eight hundred years ago, Francis saw all creation as a great family and called the sun his "brother" and the moon his "sister." A renewed appreciation of the

> value of patience could only prove beneficial for ourselves and for others. … Patience … sustains our hope and strengthens it as a virtue and a way of life. May we learn to pray frequently for the grace of patience, which is both the daughter of hope and at the same time its firm foundation. (*Spes Non Confundit*, 4)

Reflecting on patience is a great help when reviewing our own behavior. It is important, however, to overcome the misunderstanding that sees patience as a kind of passive expectation resulting from weakness of character. This is far from the case. Since ancient times, patience has been defined as "holding on," "resisting," and "staying alive." Plato and Aristotle, just to give a couple of examples, see it as an attitude of "stability," the fruit of personal effort to respect one's own dignity.

Sacred Scripture speaks openly of God's patience toward his people who are slow to believe in him. The patience of Job, the man tested to the extreme, has become the stuff of proverbs. His patience consists of a superhuman resistance to evil and to the trials that he unjustly suffers. Job's experience of pain is reflected in mankind's experience through the ages. Job's patience is far from being a passive acceptance of trials. It is an insistent request for justice and for answers to the cause of his suffering. Of course, the suffering which Job experiences leads him to depression and the edge of near-total despondency. His tenacity even pushes him to challenge God. After having lived his entire life according to the Law, he implores the Almighty to answer him (cf. Jb 31:35). As we know, God did indeed respond to Job, and his patience led him to a direct encounter with the Lord: "I had heard you only by hearsay, / but now … I have seen you with my own eyes" (42:5).

The most convincing reference to Job's patience is offered by the apostle James when he writes: "Indeed, those who had perseverance are the ones we call blessed. You have heard of the perseverance of Job and have come to understand the Lord's purpose in this respect, because the Lord is merciful and compassionate" (Jas 5:11). Similarly, Paul invites Christians to be patient, especially in the face of persecution, maintaining that such trials are merely a prelude to the certainty of hope. The apostle gives an example of patience in his own life when he carried out his ministry in the midst of great difficulties: "In everything we do we present ourselves as ministers of God: in steadfast perseverance; afflictions, hardships, and distress; in floggings, imprisonments, and riots; in labors, sleepless nights, and fasts" (2 Cor 6:4–5). A patience devoid of hope, however, would be baseless and empty in and of itself, because it would not keep its eyes fixed on the resurrection of Christ who conquers all suffering.

In many ways patience is a virtue we are called to exercise even in our own day. God is patient with us and gives us time to discover the importance of conversion towards him. Of course, good and evil continue to coexist and battle against each other, but the Christian is certain that this fight is unequal. Good will always win out in the end. Patience plays a vital role here in showing us how to wait — while still continuing to fight. Wars may continue in the world and violence will sometimes seem to have the upper hand, but Christian patience clings to the certain hope of God's intervention.

In the internet age, impatience is more common than ever. As soon as you turn on your computer or want to connect to the internet, everything seems to take too long! We no longer have the patience to wait, so caught up are we in the frenzied desire to see and do everything immediately. Life, however, is a great teacher. Even if we don't experience patience in the context of faith, nature will sooner or later impose its will on us and from that there is no escape.

The call to cultivate patience, therefore, in addition to being an invitation to grasp the value of hope, is also a challenge to those who are disillusioned, tired, and depressed. Patience, in these circumstances, challenges us not only to trust in ourselves and our own strength, but also to open our hearts and minds to the true hope that does not disappoint. It is patience that invites us to shake off the limits of self-reliance, and to awaken the best qualities we possess, because good is possible and can be achieved. Hope allows patience to fly high and banishes the laziness of those who have become numb and incapable of experiencing a sense of wonder.

Hope leads to salvation

To live the Jubilee year well, we must delve deeper into the virtue of hope and make use of it for the pastoral renewal of our communities. We are so used to talking about faith and charity that we have forgotten all about hope. This should come as no surprise — hope is the great empty gap in our preaching and catechesis. This forgetfulness of hope is a dangerous forgetfulness because it diminishes the importance of one of the most fundamental contents of the faith — namely, resurrection and eternal life. A comparison between the concept of hope in ancient thought and how we see it today immediately highlights the essential difference in Christian hope. It is not without good reason that the apostle, several times in his letters, refers to the pagans as being "without hope" (Eph 2:12), while, for us, "a better hope is introduced through which we draw nearer to God" (Heb 7:19). The apostle has before him the world of Greco-Roman antiquity, which lived with great uncertainty about the future, and therefore their idea of hope is mixed with fear, which is why young people seem to have more of it compared to older people.

The messianic hope of the Old Testament develops — albeit with exceptions — on a horizontal plane, linked to a promise that is still to be fulfilled. Christian hope, however, is based on the event of the Resurrection and on the certainty that man, in his profound unity of body and soul, can obtain salvation. Hans Urs von Balthasar rightly wrote:

> This hope that bases itself and entrusts everything to the revelation of the resurrection of the Lord, therefore also demands the greatest sacrifice from man: He must give the word of the Resurrection a weight greater than anything else, even when this word is not fully understood. Christ thus demands from man a greater renunciation than he is naturally able to bear, a stronger faith than he can express on his own, a bolder hope than the boldest hope a man could ever conceive. … He who hopes gives himself the right to try and determine all that is to come, his hope has within it something of the same character as faith and love; between these three virtues a kind of mutual inhabitation reigns. Thus, hope is an essential constitutive element of faith. Therefore, the same certainty we find in faith can be appropriated to it. (*Teodramatica*, vol. V, *The Last Act*).

All of this is possible because hope is based on the resurrection of Christ, which is not an event of the past, but carries on to this day with the strength of the Spirit, which renders it continually effective.

Charles Péguy was not entirely wrong when, in his famous story about hope, he identified it as the younger sister whom no one talks about or notices because she is hidden behind the skirts of her two older sisters, faith and charity. Yet, people of faith have an immense need for hope, especially in this difficult period of history. The French writer thinks of hope as being born on Christmas day, but it is perhaps more appropriate to say that she becomes visible in all her beauty on the day of Easter.

The liturgy, with its Sequence, has, since the eleventh century, given voice to this announcement of joy when it has Mary, the first witness of the Resurrection, say, "Christ, my hope is risen."

Revisiting Péguy's text can be not only interesting, but more importantly it can serve as an encouragement to grasp the profound meaning hidden in the story:

> Faith does not surprise me. … Charity, it goes without saying. … Faith is a faithful Bride. Charity is a Mother. But Hope is just an ordinary little girl. She came into the world on Christmas Day last year. … Yet, it is this little girl who will cross the world. This little girl from nothing. She alone, carrying the others, will cross wide worlds. ... Little Hope advances between her two big sisters unnoticed. … And we pay no attention to her, the Christian people only pay attention to the two big sisters. The first and the last. And we almost don't see the one in the middle. The little one, who is at school. And who walks hidden in her sisters' skirts. And we willingly believe that it is the two older ones who are holding the little one by the hand. She is in the middle. Between the other two. To help her take that bumpy road to salvation. How blind people are who don't see that it is the one in the middle who is pulling along her older sisters behind her. And that without her they would be nothing. For they are two elderly women. Two women of a certain age. Tired out by life. It's she, the little one, who pulls everything along. Because Faith only sees what is already there. But she [Hope] sees what is still to come. Charity loves only what is already there. But she — Hope — she loves what is still to come. God gave us hope. He began the process. He hoped that even the most infamous of sinners would try at least a little to obtain their own

> salvation. Even if only in some small way, maybe they would try a little bit. He hoped in us. Will it be said of us that we did not hope in him? God has placed his hope, his poor hope in each of us, in the lowest of us sinners. Will it be said that we, the lowest of sinners, will be the ones who will not place our hope in him? God has entrusted us with his Son … God has entrusted us with our salvation, the care of our salvation. He has made our salvation dependent on us and on him, the Son, and also on hope itself; so, should we not place our hope in him? (*The Portico of the Mystery of the Second Virtue*)

Hope, therefore, leads to salvation. And that is not all. The French poet underlines how much God himself has placed hope in each of us, especially in sinful man. Paul's text comes to mind: "May the God of hope fill you with all joy and peace in believing, so that you grow rich in hope by the power of the Holy Spirit" (Rom 15:13). It seems strange, but the apostle is not afraid to speak of God in terms of hope. The verse in question is found in the conclusion of the Letter to the Romans. The writer reminds the first Christians that Christ is salvation for all, Jews and pagans alike. And he lets slip that the latter, being the weakest, are in some sense the privileged recipients of redemption. With his faithfulness and mercy, Jesus made the face of the Father visible, and this allows the baptized person to express thanksgiving and praise to God for the work he accomplished in Christ. In this context Paul uses the expression "God of hope" as if to suggest that those who believe in Christ need to grow in hope. In the immediately preceding verses he had spoken of the "God of perseverance" (15:5), a concept closely linked to that of hope because, as has been seen previously, it indicates the attitude of waiting for the glorious return of the Lord. Here, however, the apostle allows us to go further by explaining how to practice hope so that it reaches its fullness; indeed, its superabundance.

Joy and peace are the first two things the apostle mentions because they both express hope and, in some sense, derive from hope. Both, however, need to be preserved in faith so that hope can overflow and burst forth, granting the community in Rome certainty in their choice of life and creating communion among believers. Sharing both the same faith and the life of charity that the community is called to makes their hope for salvation come alive. The hope the apostle writes about, however, is not abstract. Joy and peace are proof that it is something concrete and tangible when it is experienced. Joy and peace, therefore, are not emotional states, but real gifts offered by the God of hope, so that the kingdom of God may be made concrete and visible.

That phrase "God of hope," however, does not only indicate that at the origin of this virtue there is the action of the Holy Spirit operating in believers and offering everyone the certainty of salvation. The expression can also be interpreted, in a more nuanced sense, as the "*God who hopes.*" Von Balthasar's question remains fully valid:

> Isn't there to be found first of all, a kind of hope of the Father and the Spirit in the success of the mission of the Son? And isn't there also to be found, since God has provided man with such a precarious freedom, the hope of God that, in the end, man too will be saved (through the action of the Son, which could of course always be refused)? (*Teodramatica*, vol. V, *The Last Act*)

Why deny this possible interpretation of the Pauline text? Just as God loves, God also hopes that the revelation of the Son will be welcomed, and humanity saved. His is certainly a different kind of hope from ours, but seeing God as Jesus describes him in the parable of the prodigal son, we can see the same features present.

The father in the parable awaits the return of his son. He is far from indifferent to the boy leaving home, knowing well the dangers to which his young son's inexperience could lead. His hope for the son's return is evident in his spontaneous joy when he sees him returning home from afar. The parable does not tell us what happens to the second son who refuses to enter the house to celebrate his brother's return. It leaves the ending open for us to ponder. Yet, even in this case the logic of the parable leads us to conclude that the Father hopes both for his younger son's return and also for the older son's reconciliation with the younger brother. The "God of hope," therefore, is not extraneous to the fate of humanity; on the contrary, he hopes constantly in that humanity. He continuously acts through the Holy Spirit so that hope may transform people's hearts and thus make them capable of welcoming the gift of salvation brought about by the paschal mystery of Christ.

So it is that we must remain "steadfast" (Col 1:23) in hope, in order that the Gospel which has been proclaimed to us can grow within us to its fullness. This will be possible to the extent that, as the author of the Letter to the Hebrews reminds us, we are able to maintain "the confession of our hope without wavering, for the one who made the promise is trustworthy" (10:23).

The duel between death and life

The announcement of Christ's resurrection as the victory over death is the original source of Christian hope. We can confirm this by considering our own personal existence when faced with the drama of death. The period we live in has removed the "drama" of death from everyday life. I noticed this very clearly one summer back in the mid-1980s, while in Aberdeen, in the northeast of Scotland, providing pastoral cover for the Catholic chaplain of the city's university, Father Bill Anderson. On my regular walks, I noticed that, to my great amazement, the historic cemetery close to the city center had become a park where people strolled and went for picnics. Young couples sat on benches next to the graves, kissing and holding hands, while boys enjoyed a game of football, and no one seemed even to notice if their ball occasionally hit a tombstone. No one seemed to realize that this was a cemetery full of poor dead souls who probably only got any peace at night. The whole notion of death had been erased from the scene.

Revisiting the text of Vatican II can help us explore more deeply the theme of life and death. In the Pastoral Constitution on the Church in the Modern World, *Gaudium et Spes*, the council fathers wrote:

> It is in the face of death that the riddle of human existence grows most acute. Not only is man tormented by pain and by the advancing deterioration of the body, but even more so by a dread of perpetual extinction. He rightly follows the intuition of his heart when he abhors and repudiates the utter ruin and total disappearance of his own person. He rebels against death because he bears in himself an eternal seed which cannot be reduced to sheer matter. All the endeavors of technology, though useful in the extreme, cannot calm his anxiety; for prolongation of biological life is unable to satisfy that desire for higher life which is inescapably lodged in his breast.
>
> Although the mystery of death utterly beggars the imagination, the Church has been taught by divine revelation and firmly teaches that man has been created by God for a blissful purpose beyond the reach of earthly misery. In addition, that bodily death from which man would have been immune had he not sinned will be vanquished, according to the Christian faith, when man who was ruined by his own doing is restored to

> wholeness by an almighty and merciful Savior. For God has called man and still calls him so that with his entire being he might be joined to him in an endless sharing of a divine life beyond all corruption. Christ won this victory when he rose to life, for by his death he freed man from death. Hence to every thoughtful man a solidly established faith provides the answer to his anxiety about what the future holds for him. At the same time faith gives him the power to be united in Christ with his loved ones who have already been snatched away by death; faith arouses the hope that they have found true life with God. (18)

The bull announcing the Jubilee seems to echo this conciliar text: "The reality of death, as a painful separation from those dearest to us, cannot be mitigated by empty rhetoric" (*Spes Non Confundit*, 20). Death remains as the ultimate threat to our existence. When it directly touches a person because they experience it up close, its real drama is evident. Violent detachment seems even more irrational, and it is hard to resign oneself to such an experience. We find ourselves weak, helpless, and unable to do anything — no matter how much we may own or possess — about the face of death. Death is the ultimate enigma to be faced, but we are often left speechless when we come up against it and a feeling of emptiness seems to reign supreme. Blaise Pascal's words come to mind with their provocative sting: "The last act is bloody, however great the rest of the show may be. In the end they throw a few shovelfuls of earth on your head and it's over forever" (*Pensées*, ed. Léon Brunschvicg).

It is widely acknowledged that in today's world, death, especially violent death, has become such a staple of TV shows that it often leaves us unmoved. The deaths we see on our screens, however, despite being so numerous and different, all lead to the same conclusion. We know that we must die even if we go on trying to fool ourselves that it will never happen. It can be compared to a game of chess, as Ingmar Bergman's 1957 film, *The Seventh Seal*, so powerfully portrayed. The game may be fixed, but, in the end, checkmate arrives and the game of life ends.

Two visions of death seem to be in conflict in the history of human thought. The first is that represented by the death of Socrates. In *Phaedo* ("On the Soul"), Plato gives voice to a vision of death that is so idealized that it doesn't even seem like death at all. The philosopher, who considers the body as the prison of the soul, speaks of death as a liberation and as the culmination of the process of purification of the soul, which — via death — detaches itself from matter. Socrates remains undaunted in the face of death; there are no expressions of fear. The philosopher seems determined to reach the moment of death as though it were the definitive point of arrival for him and the only way he will be able to contemplate the truth. Rereading his last words, as reported by his young friend Phaedo, helps us understand his state of mind. To Crito (who asked him to wait for the sun to set before drinking the hemlock, and to live like other men who eat and drink what they want and "take pleasure with whoever they wish") Socrates replies:

> For those of whom you speak, Crito, it comes naturally to do as you say: They see such things as a great gain for them. But I'm right in not acting this way, because by drinking a little later I don't think I gain anything and indeed I make myself look ridiculous in my own eyes, clinging to life and skimping when there's nothing left. … I heard that life should end with voices wishing you good luck. So be calm and strong. … Crito, we owe a cockerel to Asclepius; don't forget to give it to him. (Plato, *Phaedo*, LXV–LXVI)

For Christians, the vision is different, because they believe in the fundamental union of the body with the soul; one cannot live without the other because they were created for each other in a unique and indissoluble way. Furthermore, for the believer, death represents the ultimate consequence of sin and therefore the end point of the destruction and disorder which is also seen in creation and of which man feels an integral part.

The death of Jesus is opposite to that of Socrates. Death by crucifixion, in addition to being the most ignoble, was considered the most painful and atrocious form of execution. Jesus, however, goes through it with love, giving his life for the salvation of all. His is a love that knows no comparison and which, over time, has become the archetype of every true and genuine love. Death is thus defeated by its own worst enemy: love.

The Song of Songs rightly ends with the victory of love over death when it proclaims, "Love is as strong as death" (Song 8:6). Here lies the raison d'être of Christian love, which unites the mystery of death and the mystery of love. Fear of the former gives way to the fascination of the latter, which conquers all because it will remain forever (cf. 1 Cor 13:8–13). As the apostle succinctly puts it, "The wages of sin is death, but the gift freely given by God is eternal life in Christ Jesus our Lord" (Rom 6:23).

In short, no one escapes death; it is the only thing that discriminates against no one. The reproach that Wisdom addresses to God, "Why have you put the sense of eternity in us?" (cf. Eccl 3:11), persists in all its provocative power; and though we might like to be around to see the centuries pass, that is not our destiny. Death, therefore, follows us and awaits us, though we do not know where or when. The culture of today tends to blank out our appointment with death, seeing it as something that happens to others, and therefore, until we are personally involved, it doesn't affect us. Being totally resigned to death, however, would not be fully human either, because it would prevent us from fighting this "enemy" that hangs over us until the end. Therefore, hope seems an appropriate response to this dichotomy, offering us the opportunity not to be a victim, but rather a winner. This is why Easter resonates so much with us as the great feast of hope.

Life beyond death

Charity hopes for all things (cf. 1 Cor 13:7). In the "hymn to charity," as this text is usually defined, the apostle once again relates *agape* to hope. His conviction is that love allows hope to look to the future with greater confidence and positivity. But we must examine Paul's entire theology to find the most salient references to Christian hope. Speaking of Abraham, the apostle writes that he "hoped against hope" (Rom 4:18) in God, who "gives life to the dead and calls into being what does not exist" (v. 17). It is on these words, one might say, that Christian hope is founded. Faced with the drama of death, the believer hopes — against all evidence to the contrary — that God gives life. The Christian lives by this certainty, by placing his full trust in Jesus Christ who experienced the dark night of death, but also the bright morning of resurrection.

As we know, Jesus' entire earthly existence is a journey of entrusting himself to the Father and to his will. The Gospel texts, especially those of Saint John, constantly reiterate this unique dimension of the relationship of Jesus as Son of God to the will of the Father. The key expression, "My food is to do the will of the one who sent me, and to accomplish his work" (Jn 4:34), states in no uncertain terms the meaning of Jesus' existence. It is a freely taken life decision that finds expression in many moments of Jesus' existence: from the temptation in the desert, which anticipates the drama of the Passion, to the Easter banquet, passing through the experiences of suffering and death. The life of Jesus is a revelation of his total entrustment to the Father, knowing that this path alone would lead to salvation for humanity.

Pope Francis' *Spes Non Confundit* reiterates the vision of the apostle who interprets the death of Jesus as the fulfillment of his revelation of love. The pope's interpretation is offered in the context of the light of hope:

> Saint Paul gives us much to reflect upon. We know that the Letter to the Romans marked a decisive turning point in his work of evangelization. Until then, he had carried out his activity in the eastern part of the Empire, but now he turns to Rome and all that Rome meant in the eyes of the world. Before him lay a great challenge, which he took up for the sake of preaching the Gospel, which knows no barriers or confines. The Church of Rome was not founded by Paul, yet he felt impelled to hasten there in order to bring to everyone the Gospel of Jesus Christ, crucified and risen from the dead, a message of hope that fulfills the ancient promises, leads to glory, and grounded in love, does not disappoint.
>
> Hope is born of love and based on the love springing from the pierced heart of Jesus upon the cross: "For if while we were enemies, we were reconciled to God through the death of his Son, much more surely, having been reconciled, will we be saved by his life" (Rom 5:19). That life becomes manifest in our own life of faith, which begins with baptism, develops in openness to God's grace, and is enlivened by a hope constantly renewed and confirmed by the working of the Holy Spirit. (2–3)

Death unites Jesus to every person throughout time; the apostle points to this when he writes: "For he was crucified in weakness, but he is now alive by the power of God. Similarly, we are weak in him, but in dealing with you we will live in the power of God" (2 Cor 13:4). Weakness and power alternate to express the condition of the individual person and that of faith, respectively. We know that in baptism the Christian participates in the death and resurrection of Christ, descending into the waters to free himself from weakness and rising from that source with the power of God's life in him. Being incorporated into Christ and receiving the gift of the Holy Spirit bear witness to the new life received which is strengthened by the certainty of the hope offered by the mystery of Christ's redemption.

As the author of the Letter to the Hebrews writes, Christ has become "the source of eternal salvation for all who obey him" (5:9). To achieve this, however, Christ became the perfect example of how one must fight through suffering and death with the courage that comes from the hope of abandoning oneself to the love of the Father. "We desire that each of you will show the same diligence until you have achieved the ultimate fulfillment of your hope" (Heb 6:11). This confident act of abandonment to love is Christian hope in action — it fails in nothing but conquers all because it is supported by the presence of the Holy Spirit who infuses love into a life that will never end. Those moments of insecurity, often present in daily life, should be overcome by hope — a hope supported by love. From time to time, this manifests itself as *humility* in knowing how to accept oneself; at other times as the *audacity* of knowing how to trust in God; or again as sincere *abandonment* to God's will, which, in any case, is always an expression of his love for us. Building one's life on the rock of hope, therefore, is possessing the certainty of love that has no end, and which cannot be limited by death. Only by being anchored in this love can we have the certain hope that nothing and no one can separate us from God's love, which ultimately manifests itself in our salvation.

Christian salvation is a life of communion with the Trinity. This is why we profess "eternal life" and carry within us the signs of that life beginning with baptism. This short phrase, especially when used in the profession of faith, sums up the entire content of Christian hope; for this reason, "eternal life" is interchangeable with the "kingdom of God" and with the "vision of God" which the New Testament texts repeatedly speak of. "Come, you who are blessed by my Father, inherit the kingdom prepared for you from the foundation of the world" (Mt 25:34), is not only the conclusion of a parable, but is also part of the promise that the Lord wanted to make to those who would believe in him and live by the works of mercy. In the same way, the various reminders of the apostle, according to which we will see God "face to face" (1 Cor 13:12), are an invitation to believe and hope that we will always live in his presence in the communion of love. Eternal life is not primarily a question of time, but rather it refers to the essence of existence in all its fullness, indeed in its fulfillment.

Pope Francis's explanation within the bull of why a baptistery is often built in an octagonal shape hints at the great mystery of Christian existence: a life that is already "eternal" because it is based on the mystery of the Trinitarian love of God who gives his life:

> It is worth reflecting, in the context of the Jubilee, on how that mystery has been understood from the earliest centuries of the Church's life. An example would be the tradition of building baptismal fonts in the shape of an octagon, as seen in many ancient baptisteries, like that of Saint John Lateran in Rome. This was intended to symbolize that baptism is the dawn of the "eighth day," the day of the Resurrection, a day that transcends the normal, weekly passage of time, opening it to the dimension of eternity and to life everlasting: the goal to which we tend on our earthly pilgrimage. (*Spes Non Confundit*, 20)

To understand the "novelty" of the Christian message, we must bravely take to heart Paul's text to the Corinthians, which speaks so powerfully of our own doubts about eternal life. The apostle's advice is especially true for us today: "If it is for just this life that we have hoped in Christ, we are the most pitiable of all men" (1 Cor 15:19). Paul could not have said it more clearly. If our hope relies only on the hopes offered by science and technology which, while providing some certainty, can easily deceive and certainly do not offer salvation, then we are to be pitied. Pitied because then we would be in no way different from those without faith.

We must embrace every aspect of Saint Paul's message:

> Now if Christ is proclaimed as raised from the dead, how can some of you say that there is no resurrection of the dead? If there is no resurrection of the dead, then Christ has not been raised. And if Christ has not been raised, our preaching is useless, and so is your faith. We are even false witnesses to God, for we testified that he raised Christ when he did not raise him up, assuming it is true that the dead are not raised. For if the dead are not raised, then Christ has not been raised. And if Christ has not been raised, your faith is without any foundation, and you are still in your sins. Then those also who have fallen asleep in Christ are utterly lost But Christ has been raised from the dead, the firstfruits of those who have fallen asleep. For since death came into the world through a man, the resurrection of the dead has also come through a man. Just as in Adam all die, so all will be brought to life in Christ, but each one in proper order: Christ the firstfruits; afterward, at his coming, those who belong to Christ. Then comes the end, when he hands over the kingdom to God the Father, after he

> has destroyed every sovereignty and authority and power. For he is destined to reign until he has put all his enemies under his feet. The last enemy to be destroyed is death. For God has put all things in subjection under his feet If the dead are not raised, "Let us eat and drink, / for tomorrow we die." Listen, I will tell you a mystery. We shall not all fall asleep, but we shall all be changed in an instant, in the twinkling of an eye, at the sound of the last trumpet. For the trumpet will sound, and the dead will be raised imperishable, and we will be changed. For this perishable body must be clothed with the imperishable, and this mortal body must put on immortality. When this perishable body puts on imperishability, and this mortal body puts on immortality, then will the words that are written be fulfilled: "Death has been swallowed up in victory." (1 Cor 15:12–18, 20–25, 32, 51–54)

It is not possible here to go into the richness of this text in detail. Paul's teaching, however, remains highly relevant for today's Christians who are subjected to so much confusion and uncertainty about the central tenet of their faith. As can be seen, the apostle states that it is absurd to believe in the resurrection of Christ and deny the resurrection of those who believe in him. The consequences of this contradictory stance would be catastrophic, because they would lead, first, to denying the very resurrection of Christ; then to the abandoning of the fundamental content of the announcement and preaching of the apostles, leading to the denial of the faith. The new life obtained from the paschal mystery of the Lord requires the patience to wait, and that entails a coherent lifestyle. If the resurrection of Christ and our unity with this mystery were removed, all that would remain is to become part of a culture which offers us only the here and now, and the ephemeral notion of "let us eat and drink," which is the denial of all hope. The life of the resurrection involves a true transformation of ourselves, a new type of body which, from being terrestrial (*psykikòn*) is made spiritual (*pneumatikòn*), representing our new life in the definitive entry into the kingdom of God.

Eternal life has already begun, and for the believer this involves waiting. The first believers understood this well, by making the invocation "Come, Lord Jesus, *Marana-thà*" their own (cf. 1 Cor 16:22; Rv 22:20). But the confident awaiting for the new heavens and the new earth does not lead the Church to forget that it lives in the world of history. Separating the hope for true life from the commitments required by faith would be disastrous. Hope does not paralyze the present but provides it with proper direction and a goal. Jesus will certainly return, but *when* is established by the Father, not by men. Our encounter with the Lord, moreover, happens daily and in every moment, we have the freedom and clarity to be able to recognize him in the various circumstances of life. The witness of faith, hope, and charity happens in the here and now wherever we are called to live. The present day, despite its difficulties and contradictions, still has many positives, and the Church must work to ensure that this dignity of daily existence is properly understood.

It is undeniable that we have "fallen asleep" while waiting for the Lord's return, paying excessive attention to the present. Perhaps this is because of a weakness in our faith. However, working to bring about the transformation of the world acquires its true value and meaning when faith-inspired activity is carried out in expectation of the Lord's return. There is no alternative, otherwise our testimony and liturgical prayer (which is itself imbued with hope) would become ineffective and devoid of its salvific value.

It is essential therefore that the theme of the *history of salvation* be experienced in all its existential significance. Our history needs to be reconsidered and seen once more as a *history of salvation*. Only by this change in attitude can faith be reinvigorated, can hope regain its central place, and charity open up toward ever broader horizons. The cross and resurrection of Christ do not belong to the past but are constantly present in daily life, and this is a something we cannot afford to ignore. The wait for the glorious return of the Lord to hand everything back to the Father must not find believers frightened and asleep, but rather awake and vigilant.

The anchor of hope

With good reason, symbolism and art have often been used to express hope in a broader and more profound way. The author of the Letter to the Hebrews is the first to portray hope as an anchor — an anchor provides security and stability because it guarantees shelter in a haven. "We who have taken refuge in his protection have been strongly encouraged to grasp firmly the hope that has been held out to us. We have this hope as the anchor of the soul" (Heb 6:18–19).

Art has gone to great lengths to depict hope. It is easier for art to represent faith and charity; hope is more difficult to convey since it does not evoke such an immediate emotional response as the other virtues. The image of the anchor, however, opens interesting insights, although it is almost impossible to find a reference to it in scriptural commentaries and dictionaries. Nothing is found in the classic book by J. Daniélou, *Les symboles chrétiens primitifs*; nor in the analytical *Theologisches Wörterbuch zum Neuen Testament*, precisely because the metaphor is not present in the sacred texts except on one occasion (cf. Acts 27:29, 30, 40). In this case the sacred author speaks of the anchor in a literal and not symbolic sense. This is not surprising given that, unlike the Romans and Greeks, Israel was not a people of navigators and reference to such nautical imagery was alien to them.

The Letter to the Hebrews expresses hope and trust that those who read it might set out on a safe journey toward salvation, accompanied by the hope that does not disappoint because God is faithful. The author's intention is to encourage all of us to share the same trust in the fulfillment of God's promises, because — just as he did with Abraham — so, too, God made a promise to us:

> When God made his promise to Abraham, since he had no one greater by whom to swear, he swore by himself. And so, after waiting patiently, [Abraham] obtained the promise. Human beings swear by someone greater than themselves, and the oath given as confirmation puts an end to all argument. Likewise, when God desired to show even more clearly to the heirs of his promise the unalterable nature of his purpose, he confirmed it by an oath. Therefore, by these two unchangeable acts in which it was impossible for God to lie, we who have taken refuge in his protection have been strongly encouraged to grasp firmly the hope that has been held out to us. (6:13, 15–18)

The sacred author's reasoning is extremely coherent. He insists that God's oath expresses his firm will to carry out his promises. The oath, therefore, is quite simply a further guarantee that believers possess the certainty of their hope. It is in this context, where it is made clear that human beings will be forever subject to the vicissitudes of life and need to seek refuge in God that the symbol of the anchor appears. It becomes an image of how one can cling to God and his promise. It is qualified by two adjectives, *safe* and *firm*, which commend us not to fear adversity but to be strong in the certainty that is offered.

The image of the anchor, however, allows us to reflect on the originality of our faith. It is a symbol not found in other cultures, but which has been present as a Christian symbol since the first century. Apostolic preaching, as seen previously, had given great importance to the certainty of salvation obtained from the death and resurrection of Christ. It is from this teaching that the authors of the second century began to find in the anchor the most coherent image to give meaning to the kerygma. Research seems to confirm that the anchor symbol is not used by other cultures in the way it is used in Christianity, which allows us to conclude that Christianity was first to use the anchor as a symbol of hope. "The anchor as a symbol is of purely Christian origin. There are no known pagan monuments prior to, or contemporary with, the origin of Christianity on which this figure appears as a symbol of a religious or funereal idea" (J. P. Kirsch, "Ancre," in *Dictionnaire d'Archéologie chrétienne et de Liturgie*).

We must visit the catacombs of Priscilla to see firsthand the great symbolic value entrusted to the anchor. "Among the epitaphs published so far from Priscilla's catacomb, there are around seventy which show the image of the anchor, sometimes alone, at other times accompanied by symbols, above all the fish and the palm," Kirsch's dictionary entry adds. "The origins relate to the period of the Christian consul Manius Acilius Glabrio from the end of the first century. The anchor on its own appears most frequently in the inscriptions from the second century." It can be deduced, therefore, that the anchor as a symbol of hope dates back to the very origins of the catacombs; the same carvings can be found in the catacombs of Saints Callixtus, Domitilla, and elsewhere.

Why is the anchor used? Scholars have not come up with a definitive answer, but rather they offer working hypotheses. Some have suggested that preachers found in this sign a way of depicting the participation of deceased believers in the kingdom of God following a sea journey, and the peace acquired there.

What remains beyond question, however, is that the anchor is the most ancient symbol among all the other Christian epitaphs. Even more interesting, from a theological perspective, are the changes made to the shape and form of the anchor over the years. In its earliest form, it is sculpted in a cruciform shape attesting to the salvation brought by Jesus' death on the cross.

Even more significantly, however, is the association of this symbol with that of the fish. The term *fish*, in Greek, is rendered ιχθυς. This acrostic was used by the first Christians to affirm the truth of faith: *Jesus Christ, Son of God, Savior*. In this way, the anchor became a symbol of the profound link between the salvation of the dead and faith in Jesus Christ. It must be added, however, that the symbol of the fish had a powerful Eucharistic sense, too. It also expressed the nourishment that Jesus gave to the disciples. In this context, the Christians of the first centuries spoke of the Eucharist as "medicine for immortality" and as an "antidote to avoid dying." We can find clear evidence of this in St. Ignatius of Antioch's letter to the Ephesians, where at the conclusion he writes:

> If Jesus Christ shall graciously permit me through your prayers, and if it be his will, I shall, in a second little work which I will write to you, make better known to you the new man, Jesus Christ, in his faith and in his love, in his suffering and in his resurrection. Especially if the Lord makes known to me that you come together through grace, in one faith and in Jesus Christ, who was of the seed of David both the Son of man and the Son of God, so that you obey the bishop and the presbyters with an undivided mind, breaking one bread, which is the medicine of immortality, and the antidote to prevent us from dying, but rather live forever in Jesus Christ. (Ignatius, *To the Ephesians*, XX, 1–2)

Viewed in this context, the anchor expressed hope in the immortality offered by the Resurrection. Its meaning becomes even clearer when one observes that in some epigraphs bread is added to the fish. For Christians there can be no other interpretation than a Eucharistic one. The conclusion for believers is also self-evident: The Eucharist gives us hope in eternal life.

The last aspect to consider on this topic is the association of the anchor with the dove. It seems clear that the symbolism was intended to refer to the journey of the deceased toward the eternal homeland. The presence of the dove is seen as a guarantee that the journey has come to a successful end, to the safe harbor for which the deceased person had longed. The reference here is to the dove released by Noah to check conditions after the flood, which having found a place of safety never returned to the ark (cf. Gn 8:12). The dove as a symbol of the Spirit of the Risen One further enriches the meaning because it confirms that the promise is now fulfilled. The anchor inscribed on the tombs of martyrs, accompanied by the symbol of the palm, is intended to convey that these confessors of the faith had the certainty of an unshakable hope in the Resurrection until they obtained the reward of eternal life.

An insightful comment on the symbolism of the anchor is also offered by Pope Francis:

> The image of the anchor is eloquent; it helps us to recognize the stability and security that is ours amid the troubled waters of this life, provided we entrust ourselves to the Lord Jesus. The storms that buffet us will never prevail, for we are firmly anchored in the hope born of grace, which enables us to live in Christ and to overcome sin, fear, and death. This hope, which transcends life's fleeting pleasures and the achievement of our immediate goals, makes us rise above our trials and difficulties,

> and inspires us to keep pressing forward, never losing sight of the grandeur of the heavenly goal to which we have been called. (*Spes Non Confundit*, 25)

To sum up, the theme of the anchor remains one of the most powerful symbols which Christian art has used to refer to hope. The Jubilee 2025 logo reflects this symbolism very effectively. One can see, first of all, the cruciform-shaped anchor in the foreground. The anchor is set in rough seas, a sign of the security it provides in the stormy events of life. Then there are four stylized figures to indicate humanity coming from the four corners of the earth. They hold on to each other to highlight the need for solidarity and brotherhood. The first figure, however, is clinging to the cross — the only hope on which we can truly rely. Finally, the cross is made in the shape of a sail which advances toward all God's creation to offer security and love.

2
The Language of Signs

Mankind has always lived by signs and symbols. The whole of history and each of our own personal lives could be contained within a symbol. Some like to describe life's condition as a circle, for some it is a parabola, while for others it is best expressed as a straight line. But beyond individual interpretations, this deep truth remains: Human life consists of a rich, profound, mysterious language. Man is the creator of language; indeed, he is himself a language through which he communicates what he perceives, experiences, and feels. But within our spoken language, certain elements allow us to complete what words alone cannot always express. This is what we call a "sign." A sign is the union of two elements: what is seen and what is understood but cannot always be fully expressed. When these two forms of communication come together, then we are faced with a sign. By its nature, therefore, the sign helps the mind to go beyond simple meaning, to reach the deeper truth that it expresses.

A sign, therefore, is an attempt to find a meaning we can all grasp, but which words alone are often unable to fully and completely convey. An example might help us better understand the meaning of the sign in this context: A young person falling in love for the first time feels a deep need to express his or her love. A month later, the young man in love might bring a rose to his girlfriend. Of course, he could just say to her, "I love you." He may have already done so many times, but each time it will seem to him that he has not fully expressed what is in his heart. A rose or other small gift will, in this case, be the sign of all the things he would like to have said but perhaps could never fully put into words, to convey how happy this love makes him. In short, his girlfriend — through the rose or the gift — will understand the love that is expressed to her through that sign.

In the life of faith, signs have a very real importance. The content of faith is enfolded in mystery. Much is perceived and grasped, but it can often be difficult to express the reality in words. What can we say about God using our simple forms of speech? Maybe we can babble about the mystery of God, but this is only possible because God was the first to intervene by expressing himself in human language. The same can be said about the great mystery of our salvation. Through sacramental signs, the Church allows us to grasp the salient stages of the spiritual life and thus explains the believer's journey into the life of grace. Put simply, signs are a necessary and inevitable element of personal speech. Without them, communication would be deprived of its deepest expressiveness; language would be impoverished and rendered ineffective.

The Jubilee is not unaware of this. Being a moment of particular grace, offered to believers so that they might reflect on the existence of faith and the mystery of forgiveness and reconciliation, it too must express its deepest truth through signs. For this reason, the following chapters will retrace the best-known signs of the Jubilee. It will be helpful first, however, to acquaint ourselves with them through a short introduction, to recognize their profound value and impact on our lives and the life of the Church.

Signs in Sacred Scripture

There are various signs that man creates to express his faith. A son of his time and of his culture, the Israelite never regarded the sign as something speculative. Rather, the sign was what made his concrete experience of God alive and real. For the biblical world, the sign is a manifestation of God. Since God lives in inaccessible light and no one has ever seen him, then the *sign* is best placed to express the glorious works of God among his people. It cannot be forgotten that the entire Old Testament is characterized by the command not to make any symbol or idol to represent God. The Book of Exodus states quite categorically: "You shall not make idols or any image of things that are in the heavens above" (Ex 20:4). Yet a close look at the pages of the Old Testament reveals a surprising fact: the verb "to see" occurs approximately 520 times, while the verb "to hear" crops up on no less than 1,080 occasions! It is clear that, in the biblical context, truly listening to God is much more important than trying to see him.

The story of Moses is emblematic in this context. Scripture describes Moses as the man who spoke to God "face to face, as a man speaks to his friend" (Ex 33:11). This expression indicates the relationship of great intimacy and confidence that existed between the two. Moses then addresses this unprecedented request to God: "Show me your glory!" (v. 18) — that is, let me see you! God's response helps us understand the condition of biblical man, when faced with the desire to see God:

> He answered: "I will make all my splendor pass in front of you and I will proclaim my name, the LORD, before you. I will show favor to those to whom I show favor and

> I will have mercy on those on whom I have mercy." He continued, "But you cannot see my face, for no one can see my face and live." And the LORD continued, "There is a place near me. You will stand upon the rock. When my glory passes by, I will place you in the cleft of the rock and cover you with my hand until I will have passed by. Then I will take away my hand and you will see my back, but you cannot see my face." (Exodus 33:19–23)

God, therefore, cannot be seen as long as man remains on earth; even the most privileged person cannot lay claim to having seen God.

But if we are unsure how to represent God, how can we express the faith and knowledge we have of him? The answer to this question highlights again the importance of the concept of "sign" in religion and in the experience of mystery. In fact, it is precisely here in the language of signs and symbols that we can describe our knowledge of God and his intervention in history.

One sign can be regarded as the prototype for many others: the sign of the covenant or alliance. For Israel, this sign will forever represent the intervention God made in choosing a people from among many others to be his own. A glance at the Book of Deuteronomy shows the importance of this sign of the covenant and the need for it to always remain alive and clear in people's minds:

> Ask now about the days of old, the former times. From the day that God created humans upon the earth, inquire from one end of the heavens to the other, has anything so great ever happened or has anything like it been heard of? Has any other people heard the voice of God speak from the midst of the flame, as you heard, and still live? Did God ever go and lead one nation from the midst of another nation by trials, signs, wonders, and

> battle, with a mighty hand and an outstretched arm, with great and wondrous deeds, all things that the Lord, your God, did for you in Egypt before your very eyes?
>
> You were shown these things so that you might come to know that the Lord is God; there is no other besides him. He had you hear his voice from out of the heavens so that he might instruct you. He showed you his great fire upon the earth so that you might hear his voice from the midst of the flames. It was because he loved your fathers and had chosen their descendants after them that he brought you out of Egypt before him by his great strength. He drove out greater and more powerful nations before you so that he might bring you into their land to give it to you as an inheritance, just as it is today.
>
> So today acknowledge it and take it to heart that the LORD is God in the heavens above and on the earth below. There is no other. You shall obey his statutes and the commandments that I give you today, so that all may go well with you and your children after you, and that you may live long in the land that the LORD, your God, has given you for all time. (4:32–40)

After this first sign, many more followed. They had a dual function: first, to manifest the activity of God in the lives of men; and second, to keep alive faith in him and the memory of his works. We can divide the countless signs with which the Bible presents us into three categories or contexts.

The first context is a *historical* one. Since God makes himself known through intervention in the lives of his people, it is in these moments that the signs remain indelibly fixed. The consecration to God of every firstborn is a reminder of the act of liberation accomplished while the people were slaves in Egypt (cf.

Ex 13:11–16). The liturgical feasts celebrated during the year are a sign of the great wonders performed by the strong and powerful hand of the Lord to protect Israel. In this context we must remember, first of all, the feast of Passover. It is the culmination of the history of God's choosing of the People of God and their eventual liberation by him. The extreme care with which the sacred texts refer to each celebration indicates the importance of such feasts in the life of every Israelite (Ex 12:21–28, 43–51; Dt 16:1–8). Two other feasts also held special significance: the feast of the Weeks and that of Tabernacles. The former was a celebration of the harvest, while the latter involved a pilgrimage to the Temple. Both were celebrations of joy and gladness, thanking the Lord for the harvest by offering him the first fruits of the earth.

The second context is that of *nature*. God, who had shown his power in delivering the people from bondage, was also the God who had created everything. The wonders of creation, which evoke amazement and enchantment in human hearts, become understood as signs of God's love toward his people. These same signs also recalled the great promises the Lord had made at various times in the past. It is in this context that we should reexamine three signs that recur in the pages of the Hebrew Bible: the custom of circumcision, the symbolism of the rainbow, and the stars in the sky.

Circumcision was a visible sign of a man's body, reminding him that he had been chosen by God and consecrated to him. Throughout his life, every circumcised man would know that he belonged to the People of God and had to remain faithful to them.

The sign of the rainbow recalls the biblical passage of the universal flood. Due to the repeated sins of men, God had decided to destroy his creation. Noah is chosen, "a just and blameless man at that time and he walked with God" (Gn 6:10), to build the ark and save himself from the waters of the flood. Once the devastation was over, Noah left the ark and received the promise of a new covenant. This affected the whole of humanity which, from then on, would no longer face destruction:

> God said, "This will be a sign of the covenant that I establish between me and you and every living creature for all generations. I will place my rainbow in the clouds and it will be a sign of the covenant between me and the earth. When I gather the clouds over the earth, the rainbow will appear in the clouds. I will remember my covenant between me and you and with every living creature of every kind, that water and flood shall never again destroy all flesh. The rainbow will be in the clouds, and I will look upon it and remember the eternal covenant between God and every living creature of every kind that is found upon the earth."
>
> God said to Noah, "This is a sign of the covenant that I am establishing between myself and every creature upon the earth." (Genesis 9:12–17)

Finally, the stars in the sky reminded the Israelites of the solemn promise that God had made to Abraham: "Look into the heavens and count the stars, if you can count them. Such … will your descendants be" (Gn 15:5). Whenever the believer gazed at a starry sky, it was not to take part in an astronomy lesson; rather, he would instantly recall the ancient promise made as a promise of God's faithfulness.

The final context is found in *man* himself. The experience of Israel has, in the person of its prophets, a concrete sign of the presence of God among his people. These prophets are a "voice" which continually calls people back to the covenant and to the Lord's promise, as well as acting as a "sentinel," keeping firm the hope of every Israelite. In the most difficult moments, when the destruction of the Temple, or the devastation of the country, or the deportation of the people to a foreign land might reduce trust in God, the prophet stands firm as a concrete and visible sign of the Lord's unchanging faithfulness.

Many examples of prophets as living signs can be found as we leaf through the pages of the Bible. Think of the Prophet Hosea, called in his married life to be a sign of the people's infidelity and, at the same time, of the perennial love that God has for them. The Prophet Jeremiah is a spectator and also a worker of signs that give power to his preaching: the almond branch to indicate that God watches over his word until it is implemented (cf. Jer 1:11–12); the potter who kneads the clay is a sign of the sovereignty of the Lord who can change the life of his people (18:1–10); the broken jug to recall judgment and imminent punishment (19:11); the yoke that the prophet places on his own shoulders as a message sent to the king to indicate submission (27:1–11); and, finally, the field that Jeremiah must purchase as a sign of rebuilding and of a happy future (32:1–15).

The Bible also tells of the prophet Ezekiel and various signs that he is called to work to express the will of the Lord. In his life, signs seem to abound: the sudden death of his wife; the impossibility of performing the funeral lament for her; and his being struck dumb. All these signs act as a call to verify the relationship between God and the people. In short, the prophet himself becomes a sign for Israel: "Ezekiel will be a sign for you: you shall do just as he has done. When this occurs, then you will know that I am the Lord God" (Ez 24:24).

As can be seen from this quick overview, signs are closely linked to God's revelation. Through signs, Israel recognizes the action of the Lord and his will, encounters the salvation brought about by God for her, and embraces it fully. In a way, this can be seen as a pedagogy of signs brought about by divine design. Progressively, in the multiplication of "signs and wonders" (Dt 7:19) we come to focus on the eternal sign which will never disappear because it is given by the very hand of God: "The virgin will be with child / and she will give birth to a son, / and she will name him Immanuel" (Is 7:14).

The New Testament also has its own pedagogy which makes use of signs. In light of the sign given by God himself through the incarnation of his Son, we can discern a multitude of signs that recall different aspects of Jesus' preaching. Following the custom of the times, Jesus was also asked to perform signs to prove his divine mission (cf. Mt 12:38). But Jesus refuses to respond to this request and the signs he offers are of a different kind: The sign of Jonah is to recall his freedom and the Father's plan (vv. 39–42).

It is the Gospel of John, however, which, more than the others, helps us fully understand the importance of signs in the New Testament. From the first of the signs that Jesus performs in Cana (cf. Jn 2:11), up to the "many other signs" (20:30) of which we are told at the end of the Gospel, the theme is a common thread in the entire fourth Gospel. For John, the sign is first and foremost Jesus himself. It is he who the Father sent into the world so that man might be saved by knowing God and following his teaching. Everything revolves around the person of Jesus and what he does. By seeing him, one can see the Father, because Jesus reveals his face and makes his word heard. Unlike in the past, we now can listen to God directly and see his face. The ancient commandment prohibiting representation of the divinity is cast aside, because God becomes man and allows himself to be touched, seen and heard.

Many signs radiate from Jesus that highlight both the presence within him of the kingdom of God and of the divine teaching that he reveals. One only has to think of the signs of the multiplication of the loaves (cf. Jn 6), the healing of the man born blind (9:1–40), or the resurrection of Lazarus (11:1–44) to understand the inseparable bond that unites sign and teaching.

The sign of the bread allows Jesus to affirm he is living bread; the fact that he restores sight to the blind man refers to his being "the light of the world" (Jn 9:5), while by restoring Lazarus to life, Jesus can state, "I am the resurrection and the life" (11:25). Christ, in short, is the sign placed by God in the world, and the signs that he performs begin from him and must return to him to be understood correctly and coherently.

John the Evangelist helps believers' catechetical journey by analyzing these signs. It is through them that one can recognize the glory of the son of God, and from there look to the one who is at the origin and source of Jesus' actions: the Father. The signs, in fact, are given so as to refer believers back to the Father: "The words that I speak to you I do not speak on my own. The Father who dwells in me is doing his works [signs]" (Jn 14:10). Being aware of these signs, therefore, can help us make our act of faith with greater awareness because we perceive the divinity of Jesus in them.

We cannot have a full understanding of the meaning of signs in Sacred Scripture if we do not also consider their value as teaching aids. Signs, as we have seen, are a tool allowing us to grasp a profound meaning that is otherwise hidden and which words alone cannot express. The Gospel of John allows us to better grasp this idea, as the story of the multiplication of the loaves illustrates. The evangelist says that, after the miracle, Jesus moved away from the crowd and went up the mountain to be alone for a while. Those who had seen the miracle, however, set out to look for him, wanting to proclaim him king. When Jesus saw them, he said to them, "You came for me not because you have seen signs, but because you ate the loaves and your hunger was satisfied" (Jn 6:26). This expression highlights the profound meaning that the sign possesses. One can be mesmerized by the spectacular nature of a prodigy but still not see the sign. Jesus' contemporaries were captivated by the multiplication of the loaves, but they did not want to see the deeper truth it revealed — namely, that the true and eternal food is the body of Christ.

The teaching contained in the sign is something we are always called to search out. Signs always hide a meaning, and if we do not grasp that meaning because we have marveled only at the sign itself, it means we have not properly understood the sign and not recognized it as a form of communication. When faced with a sign or miracle, we must always strive to discover what is hidden and implicit in it, and focus on the depths of meaning it contains. Jesus' reference to the sign of Jonah obliges believers not to stop at what is immediately visible but to delve deeper into the mystery. Only in this way, can the sign achieve its purpose, that of encouraging us to seek out its most profound truth.

Signs of hope

Signs have a great value even today. They are a communication tool both for daily life and the mystery of faith. Sacramental life, just to give one example, is full of the use of signs: water, oil, bread and wine, chrism, etc.; they are the language the Church uses to express the life of God in us and to strengthen our faith. In the same way, the liturgy uses various signs to help believers see a rich meaning which express the contents of the faith. The laying on of hands to indicate blessing and transmission of the Holy Spirit; the bishop's ring and crosier to recall his responsibility toward the people entrusted to him; the miter as a sign of the sanctity to which he is called — these are signs that refer to a meaning that cannot be fully expressed in words. In short, the signs used in the Church's life make use of the traditions of the past and the creativity of the present to express eternal mysteries to the people of today.

Over the centuries, the Jubilee has seen particular signs used to express the meaning and reasons behind this special time of celebration. The celebration of a Jubilee is, indeed, already a sign. It encourages believers to recognize a special moment of grace which the Church invokes from the Lord. The idea of a set time frame is an incentive to reflect on one's faith and on the responsibility to bear witness — something Christians are called to do, always and everywhere. From the first Jubilee of 1300 right through to that of 2000, certain signs remained unchanged, while others were added or modified. The celebration of the special indulgence is a permanent sign of the Jubilee, as is the notion of pilgrimage and the traditional visit to St. Peter's Basilica. The opening of the Holy Door was added later, as was the visit to the four Roman basilicas.

For the next Jubilee, *Spes Non Confundit* highlights the importance of signs in its celebration. Pope Francis has compiled a series of signs which incentivize believers not to remain passive, but to become true workers of hope. These signs allow us to approach our contemporaries more easily with a language suited to them.

The culture in which we live uses imagery as the principle means of communication. Not only that, but young people also live in a world that fascinates them precisely due to the multitude of experiences they can have. On the one hand, this proliferation is frightening because it runs the great risk of not offering the depth necessary to live the experience in a fully profound way. On the other hand, it challenges the community to embrace different experiences so that young people can find the one that attracts and interests them. Both perspectives, however, show the need for concrete signs not only to be offered, but also to be directly experienced. The invitation of the Jubilee, therefore, is not to limit ourselves to just talking about hope, but to actually put hope into practice in the places where it is most needed.

It is worth mentioning, at this juncture, a few of the signs of hope in question, which can help us get involved in the Jubilee celebrations. By embracing these signs, we can hopefully avoid just hearing the announcement of hope at a theoretical level without feeling any need for direct personal involvement.

The first sign must surely be that of peace. "Is it too much," asks Pope Francis, "to dream that arms can fall silent and cease to rain down destruction and death?" (*Spes Non Confundit*, No. 8). The Jubilee is tasked with reminding believers that those who "make peace with their hands," to translate Matthew's Beatitudes text literally, will be called children of God (cf. Mt 5:9). Peace is achievable when we live out our responsibility for the common good and become involved in activities that promote and restore peace. Of course, when faced with the violence of war, personal commitment may be more complex, but peace is not just the absence of war. As Pope Francis has recalled, it is "a general condition in which the human person is in harmony with him/herself, in harmony with nature and in harmony with others. This is peace. Nevertheless, silencing weapons and extinguishing the hotbeds of war is an inevitable condition to begin a journey that leads to peace in its various aspects" (Angelus, January 4, 2015).

The second sign of hope that Pope Francis is calling for is a full and total "yes" to life. Some might be surprised by this, but we can better understand its inclusion if we consider the global context in which it is placed. The statistics that reveal the problem of a rapidly declining birthrate should give cause for serious reflection and concern. Looking at figures for the last sixty years, it is shocking to see how the numbers are in constant decline, falling from 5.1 to 1.2 children per woman, globally. Italy, Korea, and Japan lead the negative ranking and highlight a trend toward childlessness. For a few decades, China imposed a one-child policy, but today that law is no longer required. The underlying causes behind these figures are many: from greater access to paid work for women to political policies adopted in some countries, from the increase in living costs to the delay in the age at which people get married. These conditions, which are partly solvable, have, however, at their base, a huge cultural shift: Fewer women now desire to be mothers, and those who do desire children want to have a maximum of two. It is certainly true that we are living longer, but this lack of procreation will lead to serious problems, especially economic ones, for older people. Migration cannot be used as a solution to declining birthrates, because once migrants become integrated into their new country, they find themselves with the same difficulties as other families and the desire to have fewer children. In short, we are living in a global context in which the fundamental importance of the transmission of life is no longer perceived as being a priority and the result is that we withdraw more and more into ourselves. Selfishness rears its ugly head, and the tranquility of a carefree life takes precedence over the beauty of love which generates new life. The pope's invitation should not fall on deaf ears:

> It is urgent that responsible legislation on the part of states be accompanied by the firm support of communities of believers and the entire civil community in all its components. For the desire of young people to give birth to new sons and daughters as a sign of the fruitfulness of their love ensures a future for every society. This is a matter of hope: It is born of hope and it generates hope. (*Spes Non Confundit*, 9)

The third sign of hope focuses on attitudes to prisoners, a cause which has long been close to Pope Francis's heart. He even intends to open a "Holy Door" inside a prison "as a sign inviting prisoners to look to the future with hope and a renewed sense of confidence" (10). He sees this as a particularly important gesture because he wants to show special sensitivity toward people who, despite having made mistakes, deserve a chance of redemption.

For them, hope cannot be just a word, but must take on real substance and action, leading them to proper reintegration and redemption. As in previous Jubilees, the pope speaks authoritatively to governments asking that they implement "initiatives aimed at restoring hope; forms of amnesty or pardon meant to help individuals regain confidence in themselves and in society" (10). It is well known that governments are somewhat reluctant to take on initiatives like this because they feel intimidated by possible negative reactions from some sections of society. But the voices of those who speak up for prisoners and other disadvantaged groups should not be silenced. Attention should also be paid to the conditions experienced by thousands of prisoners who are often denied dignity, as well as renewing the call for the definitive abolition of the death penalty in as strong and convincing a manner as possible. "In every part of the world, believers, and their pastors in particular, should be one in demanding dignified conditions for those in prison, respect for their human rights and above all the abolition of the death penalty, a provision at odds with Christian faith and one that eliminates all hope of forgiveness and rehabilitation" (10).

For the sick, for migrants and refugees, as well as for the "billions of the poor, who often lack the essentials of life" (15), we must act so that concrete signs of hope can be given in the belief that their conditions of life can improve. References to the common good cannot exclude those categories of people who are looking for a better future. Unfortunately, for many such people the dream of a better life for themselves and their families culminates in a dangerous journey on rough seas due to the lies and greed of ruthless men. The pope's words are timely and provocative here, too: "Their expectations must not be frustrated by prejudice and rejection. A spirit of welcome, which embraces everyone with respect for his or her dignity, should be accompanied by a sense of responsibility, lest anyone be denied the right to build a dignified existence" (13).

It is a matter of great urgency that we open our eyes to the needs of those who live in poverty and experience marginalization. Entire populations live every moment of their lives in the shadow of death. Humanity today is faced with new and more subtle forms of slavery than those known in the past. For too many people, freedom continues to be a word devoid of meaning. Many nations, especially the poorest ones, are burdened by a debt that has reached such proportions that it is practically impossible for them to pay it. It is clear, moreover, that real progress cannot be achieved without effective collaboration between peoples of every language, race, nationality, and religion. Therefore, the abuses that lead to the dominance of one over the other must be eliminated — they are a sin and the fruit of injustice. We must not forget Jesus' reminder to those who are intent on accumulating treasures only on this earth (cf. Mt 6:19) while not enriching themselves "in the sight of God" (Lk 12:21).

In short, we must create a new culture of solidarity and international cooperation, in which everyone — especially rich countries and the private sector — assume responsibility for an economic model that serves the person and his/her dignity rather than serving profit. The day must come — and come soon — when even the poor man, like Lazarus, can sit beside and share the same banquet as the rich man, rather than having to feed himself with scraps from the table (cf. Lk 16:19–31). Extreme poverty is a source of violence, resentment, scandal, and, unfortunately, death for many innocent people who dream in vain of a more humane life — a life worth living. To remedy this situation is to carry out an act of justice and is therefore the promise of a better future.

Finally, signs of hope need to be given to young and old alike. The reasons are clearly different, but the desire for hope is identical. For the former, the *Spes Non Confundit* reminds us, "we must not disappoint them, for the future depends on their enthusiasm" (12). In the case of the latter, the pope reiterates how important it is to esteem them "for the treasure that they are, their life experiences, their accumulated wisdom, and the contribution that they can still make" (14).

Young people are reminded how ephemeral and meaningless it can be "escaping into drugs, risk-taking and the pursuit of momentary pleasure" because they then run the risk of falling into "depression and even self-destructive actions" (12). These are strong words that should not be seen as mere rhetoric. Of course, we must not ignore the beauty of millions of young people who show enthusiasm, pursue the search for happiness, and demonstrate commitment to the future. The solidarity they show, as well as the joy they bring to many initiatives, makes them protagonists of true hope. Yet, a deep concern remains that we are seeing a generation in the throes of anxiety (cf. *The Anxious Generation*, a recent study and book by Jonathan Haidt). They are increasingly weakened and uncertain due to a digital culture that puts concentration, freedom, and the search for truth at risk. Recovering a genuine sense of beauty through the exercise of wonder and amazement would represent a real sign of looking to the future with the certainty of hope.

The Jubilee is a call to a conversion of heart through a change of life. It reminds everyone not to focus exclusively or give absolute importance either to the goods of the earth, because they are not God, or to the dominion (or the claim of dominion) of mankind, because the earth belongs to God and to him alone: "The land belongs to me and you are my aliens and tenants" (Lv 25:23).

3
The Jubilee Indulgence

Cardinal Charles Journet (1891–1975) wrote that "the doctrine of indulgences is a delicate but authentic flower of the ever-living tree of Christian doctrine" (*Theology of Indulgences*). Sadly, we now need to acknowledge that the delicate flower has somewhat wilted. One of the causes of this change seems to be that the doctrine of indulgences has been understood, over the centuries, in the context of sin.

A glance at the most recent definition of indulgences proposed by the *Catechism of the Catholic Church*, illustrates this very clearly. Referring to the constitution *Indulgentiarum Doctrina* of Paul VI, the *Catechism* writes: "An indulgence is a remission before God of the temporal punishment due to sins whose guilt has already been forgiven, which the faithful Christian who is duly disposed gains under certain prescribed conditions through the action of the Church which, as the minister of redemption, dispenses and applies with authority the treasury of the satisfactions of Christ and the saints" (1471). This clearly sums up the essential points of the doctrine and is complete in its own way. The mystery of Christ's redemption, the mediation of the Church, the disposition of the believer and the remission of punishment are all mentioned. Thus the essential elements of indulgences are tied together, and it is made clear that the lack of even one of these elements would cause the entire edifice to collapse.

This rather technical presentation of the doctrine found in the *Catechism* should come as no surprise to us. It is linked to a view of indulgences that refers closely to the original practice, which linked indulgences to the penitential "tariffs." These tariffs, which started in the seventh century, established the various corporal mortifications penitents were required to carry out. The history of theology clearly shows, however, that such an approach inevitably gave rise to questions that remain valid today. Indeed, this approach may have led to a certain misunderstanding of the value and meaning of indulgences in the religious practice of God's people. It is useful, therefore, to propose a better definition of the meaning of an indulgence today. The indulgence should be seen in a more coherent way, in the light of the Sacrament of Reconciliation and, consequently, in the context of God's love and mercy. In other words, it is better to focus, in the first instance, on the forgiveness of God rather than on man's sin. This distinction is significant, as are its consequences, both from a theological and a pastoral perspective.

The first indulgence

The approaching Jubilee once again brings to the fore the issue of indulgences and their celebration. Historically, the Jubilee was born in the shadow of the "great indulgence" the people of Rome asked of the pope in the thirteenth century. According to commentators of the time, the first Jubilee came about in December 1299 with the belief that, in the centenary year, pilgrims to St. Peter's Basilica would obtain a full remission of sins — that is, an indulgence. On January 1, 1300, during his Christmas octave sermon, an anonymous preacher spoke of the "*centesimo seu de iubileo*" (centenary, or jubilee, year). That afternoon the rumor quickly spread throughout the entire city. In the evening, "there was a tumultuous influx of the Roman faithful to St. Peter's to obtain this full indulgence" (A. Galuzzi, "*Gli anni santi nella storia della Chiesa*", in Aa.Vv., *Tertio millennio adveniente. Commento teologico pastorale*, Cinisello B., 1996).

The news reached Pope Boniface VIII who, for the first and perhaps only time in the history of the Church until then, promulgated the papal bull *Antiquorum Habet Fida Relatio* on February 22, 1300. The Jubilee indulgence was thus established, backdated to Christmas of the previous year. The text of this bull makes for interesting reading. In some parts it picks up on previous bulls with which the pope had granted indulgences. What is most fascinating however, is what the pope writes: "We, trusting in the mercy of almighty God, in the merits and authority of his apostles and strengthened by the opinion of our brothers, grant by virtue of the fullness of the apostolic power an indulgence of all sins, that is not only full and abundant, but very full." Some elements mentioned in these lines are worth noting because they will return as constant features in the history of indulgences. As can be seen, the mercy of God is mentioned first, followed by a reference to the holiness, apostolicity, and authority of the Church in granting forgiveness.

The Jubilee allows us to better understand the historical link between two elements in the life of the Church. The doctrine of indulgences does not originate in the Jubilee; indeed, the opposite is true … the Jubilee stems from the doctrine of the indulgence, which gives meaning to the concept of pilgrimages, and to the works of penance and charity that the pilgrim was required to carry out to obtain the "great pardon."

If we examine the second Jubilee papal bull, however, we can see that the Jubilee also brought its own contribution to the development of the understanding of indulgences. In this second Holy Year, as far as I can trace in the documents, the expression "the treasures of the Church" occurs for the first time in reference to the Jubilee indulgence, a phrase which would become a technical term in the language of this doctrine up to the present day.

The bull *Unigenitus Dei Filius* of Pope Clement VI demonstrates this amply:

> The Only Begotten Son of God redeemed us not with corruptible gold and silver, but with his own precious blood. Since then, so that the goodness of such a copious outpouring would not be rendered useless, ineffective, or superfluous, the good Father, wanting to accumulate treasures for his children, obtained for the Church militant a treasure that was greater than ever, an infinite treasure for men, by which, those who make use of it might participate in the friendship of God. This treasure was not wrapped in a handkerchief, not hidden in a field, but rather offered to be beneficially distributed to the faithful through blessed Peter, keyholder of heaven, and his successors, his vicars on earth, to be applied with mercy, for particular and reasonable causes, for a total or partial remission of the temporal punishment due for sins, both in a general and in a specific way (as they deem fit before God), in favor of those who have truly repented and confessed. In truth it is recognized that the merits of the blessed Mother of God and of all the elect, from the first to the last, contribute to the accumulation of this treasure, and there is absolutely no need to fear its exhaustion or diminution, both due to the infinite merits of Christ, and the fact that the more people who through its application are brought to justice, the more

the accumulation of the same merits grows.

The text, although relatively short, is a wonderful summary of the teaching on indulgences. Here the fundamental truths which support the doctrine are clearly stated and serve as a basic starting point for the various explanations proposed by different theological schools over the centuries.

A look back through history

The doctrine of indulgences has its own distinct history. This history deserves to be revisited — at least in its essentials — to better understand the theological developments which have taken place over the centuries. The doctrine of indulgences forms part of the penitential practice that the Church has always embraced. We know that from the first to the seventh century the remission of sins committed after baptism had a public element attached to it. To be readmitted to the community, the sinner had to demonstrate commitment to a life of penance and was required to carry out some penitential act imposed by the bishop. During this period, there was no clear distinction between the guilt of sin and the punishment due to the sin committed before God. The harsh penance imposed on the sinner was intended to indicate his or her purification before God. On this journey, however, the sinner was not alone, but was accompanied by the prayer of the community, by the supplications made by the presbyters during the liturgical celebration, and by the intercession of the martyrs. The journey of conversion and purification, therefore, was, for a long period, lived in a communitarian context.

From the seventh century to the eleventh century, what we know today as "private" penance came into use. It is this practice which places the act of contrition/reconciliation between the confession of sin and the penitential act. Indeed, this is what makes us aware of the distinction between the guilt of sin and the punishment that must be atoned for. As previously mentioned, the tariffs (the penitential books which regulated the fasts and forms of penance to be applied for each sin), were counted in days, weeks, and years, and these became the reference points which allowed the sinner to see his life being purified. In the eleventh and twelfth centuries we can see the first indulgences coming into existence. Bishops, through the intercession of the prayer of the Church, began to remit, in whole or in part, specific forms of penance which had been imposed by priests on penitents. This, however, did not happen automatically; rather, it was a kind of commutation of the imposed penance into an easier and more accessible form.

Theologians generally agree that the legitimacy and use of indulgence became established in the thirteenth century. Access to the "treasury of the Church" became an important reference point for understanding that the sinner, standing before God and seeking to purify himself with penance, did not possess the required strength to fulfill the burdens of penance imposed on him. So, the Church, as Mother of mercy, drew from the holiness of her saints the strength and merits necessary to make up for what was lacking in the sinner. In this way the gradual separation between guilt and punishment was established. The indulgence was no longer linked to the penance imposed, but to the full purification obtained before God for sins committed, and could also be applied to the deceased. The fifteenth century certainly saw this practice in operation (cf. P. Adnès, "*Indulgences*," in *Dictionnaire de Spiritualité*).

A second important milestone regarding indulgences came with the Council of Trent. On December 4, 1563, the *Decretum de Indulgentiis* was approved in which the fathers of the council defined the doctrine and refuted the criticisms raised by Lutheran reformers. "Indulgences," they affirmed "are very salutary for the Christian people" and those who think they "are useless or that they cannot be granted by the Church" (*DS*) are mistaken. The Council of Trent clarified that the forgiveness of sins, through sacramental absolution, did not automatically obtain the remission of the consequences of sin. In short, God always remains free to act as he will but grants the Church the possibility of intervening with its own practices to ensure that the forgiveness of sin can be followed by the full remission of its consequences.

Shortly after Vatican II, Paul VI promulgated the document *Indulgentiarum Doctrina* in which he offered a full explanation of the meaning of indulgences and how they should be understood and accessed by the faithful. The presentation of this document inevitably echoed the new ecclesiological insights of Vatican II. What emerged was the possibility of new understandings built on the teaching of the Council of Trent.

Essentially, the Church's role of mediation is expressed in a new and more extensive fashion. It highlights the fact that indulgences are not obtained by virtue of one's own internal dispositions, but rather as the result of a direct intervention of the Church. It is the Church which "dispenses and applies" to the faithful the fruits of her sanctity founded on the redemption of Christ. The Church, defined as the "minister of redemption," with ministerial authority *(auctoritative)*, becomes the dispenser of grace, which extends to the ultimate form of forgiveness, that which also eliminates the *consequences* of sin. The Church, therefore, strengthened by the mystery of Christ's redemption, intercedes with the Father, the only true foundation of grace, so that the sinner may obtain full and total forgiveness. The mediating role of the Church, therefore, is clearly recognized by Paul VI's apostolic constitution. It is not limited to just a prayer of intercession to the Father for the sinner, but instead becomes a true ministry of the Church, acting in full accordance with her own nature as the Body of Christ.

Trapped in a game of language?

At this point in our consideration of indulgences, a question of huge significance is bound to cross our minds. How can the doctrine of indulgences be explained to the believer of *today* who has little knowledge of the basic truths of Church teaching? Before answering that question, it is important to acknowledge two dangers that should be avoided. The first is an *absolutization* of this doctrine. It should be remembered that the doctrine of indulgences is part of a hierarchy of truths, and, therefore, it has its own dogmatic position in that classification. This position must be respected, without trying to give it a new importance that is unwarranted. On the other hand, we must avoid simply dismissing it, which would be quite unjustifiable. Indulgences are part of the heritage of ecclesial tradition and are closely connected to certain fundamental truths of revelation.

No one doubts the redemptive value of the death and resurrection of Christ, or the mediating role of the Church and her authority over mankind's sins. In the same way, faith teaches us that a life of sin entails consequences which lead man to suffering in this life or to damnation in eternal life (cf. Gn 3:16–19; Lk 19:41–44; Rom 2:9; 1 Cor 11:30). These truths form the foundation of the teaching on indulgences and constitute its essential content. The objection that "people no longer hear or understand these things" is surely superficial. In these situations, theology and pastoral care must find new forms of language to make the richness of this doctrine understood. To simply dismiss a particular element of the Church's teaching is never a good thing for the people of God nor for their life of faith.

To avoid the issue of indulgences being regarded as unimportant, but also to respond to the criticism that it represents a juridical vision of sin, the doctrine needs to be reframed. This reframing must take place in the light of a theology that puts God's mercy and forgiveness at its core. Without this contextualization the doctrine risks remaining the preserve of a closed circle of believers, and we would remain trapped in the current pointless conflict zone, where, for some, indulgences are considered an incalculable treasure of grace, while for others they are considered an embarrassing anachronism that must be gotten rid of. Therefore, we should ask ourselves what understanding the men and women of today (whether believers or not) have of phrases such as: gain an indulgence, temporal punishment, guilt, treasury of the saints, satisfaction of Christ, and so on.

The problem of understanding and communication is fundamental, especially when the language used no longer has a clear meaning in the culture and is not the language people generally speak. Overcoming the language problem, however, only allows us to postpone the solution. The problem itself remains unresolved. To help people understand and accept the doctrine of indulgences it is important to reemphasize at least three fundamental elements: the mercy of God, the reality of sin, and the mediation of the Church.

1. The first element that helps us to set the context is mercy, the ultimate sign of the Father's love which reaches the point of extreme forgiveness for the sinner. Christian life is born and develops in love. This reaches its culmination in the mystery of the death and resurrection of Christ, who obtains salvation for those who believe in him. Paul's text is very significant in this regard: "At the appointed time, while we were still helpless, Christ died for the ungodly. Indeed, it is seldom that anyone will die for a just person, although perhaps for a good person someone might be willing to die. Thus, God proved his love for us in that while we were still sinners Christ died for us" (Rom 5:6–8). This quote comes from the central part of the Letter to the Romans. The apostle has just stated that the Christian lives by hope and this does not disappoint as "the love of God has been poured into our hearts through the Holy Spirit" (v. 5). Paul is referring here

to the historical event of unmatchable importance — the death of Christ. In it we see the ultimate sign of divine love, because it surpasses every understanding of love that man could possibly imagine. It is, in fact, a death freely offered out of love for those who are still in the position of rejecting that love. This love, however, is not a mere historical fact. On the contrary, it continues to this day to effectively make visible the uniqueness of God's divine nature. This love resides in believers, deep in their hearts, and remains as a constant and perennial call to conversion toward God and growth in communion with him.

God's love, therefore, is for us. It is a love for sinners, so that they can be reconciled with the Father. The life of faith thus becomes an existence that grows in the love already "poured into our hearts." Here we are helped to understand how its application to indulgences can be seen in a positive way, as if it were a constant training program that believers undertake to help them live and grow in the love that has been placed in their hearts. In other words, the celebration of the indulgence is a way of practicing love. The reality is that, faced with the love with which Christ loves, no one can avoid acknowledging the wickedness of their own sins and the limit such sins impose on their personal existence. Of course, everyone remains a sinner and carries with them signs of their falls, but when faced with the love of Christ, one discovers that life in love is far better. In short, the sinner's punishment is lessened if life is increasingly seen as growing in love and living for love.

2. The second element is the condition of sinfulness which we all bear and which we all know only too well. We understand that the call to Christian life is a vocation to perfection: "Be perfect as your heavenly Father is perfect" always remains the goal toward which a believer strives. But our existence often seems marked more by the weight of sin than by progress toward perfection. We know temptation, we experience betrayal and falls,

and yet, alongside this, we also perceive the action of grace which urges us to conversion. The forgiveness that the Christian asks for from the Father in the Sacrament of Reconciliation is genuinely granted to him. He truly obtains forgiveness of sins, and the path of grace opens before him. Conversion, however, is not an abstract idea. Metanoia requires us to have the strength to look at the concrete reality of our existence. This is not achieved solely by the desire, obtained through forgiveness, to live according to the Gospel, but is lived out in the life story of each person, made up of thoughts and actions, of ideals and contradictions.

In short, the stains of our sinful lives are not wiped away with the rub of a sponge. They leave us with the residue that sin creates. Just as sin does not happen instantly but is the fruit of a progressive distancing from the good, so in each person's own life story there remains real contradictions which are the consequences of a life of sin. This is the "punishment" that is removed with the indulgence. Absolution, which the priest offers on behalf of Christ and the Church, effectively forgives the sins committed. In the words of the prophet, God no longer remembers them, he puts them behind him (cf. Is 55:7–9). So, the sins themselves are gone, but the effect the sins had on us remains — that discomfort and weakness which, in the end, always leads us to committing the same sins. The indulgence comes into play at this stage. God's mercy reaches deep down, even to man's most sinful tendencies, freeing him fully and inviting him to live in love rather than in the disorder of sin. In a way, it is an additional grace that is offered to choose good and reject evil.

3. But how can this come about if the individual sinner experiences within himself the limits and contradictions of sin? The answer lies in the third element: the mediation role that the Church plays in this process. It is often forgotten that sin is not only an offence against God; it is also an act that breaks ecclesial communion. This is because, through baptism, we become

members of and are in a sense inserted into the mystical body of Christ. In short, we live the Communion of Saints (*Communio Sanctorum*). The apostle Paul's teaching on this is well known: "There is one body and one Spirit, as well as one hope to which you have been called by your vocation, one Lord, one faith, one baptism, one God and Father of all, who is over all and through all and in all" (Eph 4:4–6; cf. also 1 Cor 12:12–27). The Christians brought together by the Holy Spirit form what Saint Augustine called the *Christus totus* — that is, a *mystical person* who is the Church. It is a visible and spiritual community, living on earth but already in possession of the goods of heaven. The Church should not be thought of in any sort of dualistic way. It is "one complex reality which coalesces from a divine and a human element" (*Lumen Gentium*, 8).

Thus the Church both *is* communion and works effectively to *achieve* communion. This *communio*, however, which is always a gift from God, is made up both of a communion with God and a communion between men. Thus the sacramental character of the Church emerges in all its fullness and natural reality, a character which finds its source and center in the Eucharist. We are called as believers to transform ourselves through the Eucharist, so that the mystery which we live in faith becomes visible in our lives, too. It is this life of communion which creates a relationship between believers that goes beyond the sociological dimension, extending also to those already in the promised happiness of heaven and whose number is incalculable (cf. Rv 7:9). Their life of holiness nourishes our existence in a mysterious but effective way, and comes to the aid of our weakness, allowing grace to act in us by virtue of the holiness of all. This is the "treasury of the Church." God, in his freedom, allows the goods of some to pass to others who are most in need and, in this way, the believer can fully experience the truth he professes in the Creed — namely, the Communion of Saints. It is a solidarity of love that never ends and knows no boundaries.

The indulgence as an expression of mercy

Indulgences are not the only means offered to the believer to obtain forgiveness for the consequences of sin. Among the many means available we must, first, remember charity, which Saint Peter says, "covers a multitude of sins" (1 Pt 4:8). Then there are the different forms of enduring suffering, the trials of life whether large or small. If they are lived according to the will of God, they have the same effectiveness as the indulgence. It is therefore wrong to make the topic an absolute, but it is also wrong to ignore it. Its practice, though, does lead to real benefits for the spiritual life. To quote Paul VI:

> This salutary practice teaches us in the first place how it is "sad and bitter to have abandoned … the Lord God." Indeed, the faithful, when they acquire indulgences, understand that by their own powers they could not remedy the harm they have done to themselves and to the entire community by their sin, and they are therefore stirred to a salutary humility. Furthermore, the use of indulgences shows us how closely we are united to each other in Christ, and how the supernatural life of each can benefit others so that these also may be more easily and more closely united with the Father. (*Indulgentiarum Doctrina,* 9)

Awareness of oneself as a redeemed sinner, an understanding of being part of the Body of Christ, and knowing that one is always before the goodness of the Father … these three elements summarize the real richness of indulgences of which we must not lose sight.

One final question needs to be answered: Would it be a good

idea to substitute the word *indulgence* and replace it with something else? Personally, I am not convinced. A quick assessment of the issues involved in changing the word makes clear that the problem could well be increased rather than resolved by doing so. There exists, whether we like it or not, a collective inertia that does not allow the instant adaptation of people's language and understanding. What should perhaps be encouraged, therefore is the use of the singular term: *indulgence*. In this way, the concept expressed would be more easily reconcilable with that of *mercy*.

Ultimately, the most coherent and adequate term to express the reality of indulgence is that of mercy. For it indicates the compassion and *goodness* of God, with the connotation of *paternal gentleness* toward sinful children. For some, mercy is connected to the theme of justice, which is "owed" by God in response to man's sin, but justice also has the meaning of "benevolence" toward an *unhappy person*. Who is more unhappy than the sinner who feels distant from God and who does not have the strength to ask God to be fully forgiven? If we were to express the concept of indulgence in another way, we could say that it is the mercy of God that the Church, strengthened by the mystery of Christ's redemption and its own holiness, offers to believers. This mercy is offered so that they can experience the fullness of forgiveness, forgiveness taken to its logical conclusion, in the context of an existence lived in the light of love.

Pope Francis emphasizes this when he writes in *Spes Non Confundit*: "The indulgence is a way of discovering the unlimited nature of God's mercy. Not by chance, for the ancients, the terms 'mercy' and 'indulgence' were interchangeable, as expressions of the fullness of God's forgiveness, which knows no bounds … as Saint Paul VI wrote, [Christ] 'is himself "our indulgence"'" (23).

4
The Pilgrimage

Homo viator

> My father was a wandering Aramean, and he went down into Egypt with a few people and he dwelt there becoming a great nation, powerful and numerous. The Egyptians mistreated us, afflicted us and forced us to do hard labor. We cried out to the Lord, the God of our fathers, and the Lord heard our voice and took notice of our affliction, labor, and oppression. The Lord brought us forth out of Egypt with a mighty hand and an outstretched arm, with terrifying and awesome signs and wonders. He brought us to this place and gave us a land, this land that is flowing with milk and honey. (Deuteronomy 26:3–9)

With these words the ancient Israelite professed his faith in the Lord. He recognized that God had intervened in his life through signs that he could see, recognize, and recount to others. At the beginning of his story, he identified his ancestors as being a people on the move. Following the initial wandering of the nomad searching only for better grazing for his flock, came the starting out of the people on a journey toward the promised land. This was a moment of revelation by God to his people, when he set his seal on the covenant he had made with them.

This journey extended the one which began with the call to Abraham, when the patriarch was invited to leave his father's house to go to a "country" that God would show him (cf. Gn 12:1). Abraham left, as he was instructed to, relying only on the word of the Lord. He dedicated his entire existence to God so much so that he is referred to as "the father of all believers." The life of Abraham, "our father in faith" as the liturgy states, can be seen in the context of a continuous pilgrimage toward the land that the Lord had promised him. He didn't know where he was going; but he trusted in that word that had been addressed to him at a key moment in his life, when he least expected it. God met him in his own way, not respecting the customs of men, but in a way that expressed his divine freedom.

The call was decisive, and even though he was already seventy-five years old, he questioned himself and his entire existence before setting out on the path that the Lord was showing him. We should not forget that the promise made to him, was not the easiest to believe: "Look into the heavens and count the stars, if you can count them. Such … will your descendants be" (Gn 15:5). Abraham had no children! Despite this, he set out, leaving behind all the security he had obtained, supported only by the unwavering certainty that God was with him.

The life of every Israelite was regulated by the Law which provided for three ritual pilgrimages each year, with the city of David as their destination. The Book of Deuteronomy provides a detailed description of these moments: first the Israelite would have to go to Jerusalem on the feast of Passover, for seven days, concluding with "a solemn assembly to the Lord" (Dt 17:8). A second pilgrimage had to be made at the beginning of the harvest to thank the Lord through the offering of the harvest. A third pilgrimage was held when the wheat was threshed and the grapes had been pressed in thanksgiving for the help the Lord God had given (cf. Dt 16:16).

Some of the psalms recall these moments. They are known as the "ascension psalms" because they were recited or sung while the pilgrims were going: "I rejoiced when they said to me, / 'Let us go to the house of the Lord.' / And finally our feet are standing / at your gates, O Jerusalem" (Ps 122:1–2).

It is in this spirit that every believer should begin their own pilgrimage toward the definitive encounter with the Father. Pope Francis has referred to this several times. In the programmatic letter of his pontificate, he wrote that every Christian should carry within him the dynamic of the Exodus, going beyond himself, journeying on past each stop reached along the way. He even says that "the Church's closeness to Jesus is part of a common journey" (*Evangelii Gaudium*, 23) to indicate that communion with him is a permanent journey that should not be frightening or exhausting. *Spes Non Confundit* also contains significant words on this theme:

> Pilgrimage is of course a fundamental element of every Jubilee event. Setting out on a journey is traditionally associated with our human quest for meaning in life. A pilgrimage on foot is a great aid for rediscovering the value of silence, effort, and simplicity of life. In the coming year, *pilgrims of hope* will surely travel the ancient and more modern routes in order to experience the Jubilee to the full. . . . Journeying from one country to another as if borders no longer mattered, and passing from one city to another in contemplating the beauty of creation and masterpieces of art, we learn to treasure the richness of

> different experiences and cultures, and are inspired to lift up that beauty, in prayer, to God, in thanksgiving for his wondrous works. (5)

There are certain characteristics in every pilgrimage that are worth mentioning. At least three can easily be identified: the call, the promise, and the certainty of its fulfillment. Pilgrimage as an act of faith undoubtedly starts from a personal call, when we are asked to set out and follow the path that God has laid out for each one of us. In this way, the believer makes himself available to discover the promise made to him and can grow and persevere throughout his life in the hope of its fulfillment.

Pilgrimage is not the sole prerogative of Christianity, of course. It belongs, rather, to the history of humanity. Where there is human life, there is journeying. Any analysis of the history of religions, or even a phenomenology of the sacred, would clearly show the presence of pilgrimage as a universal element. It helps relate the human to the divine, or, at least, it helps lead humanity to the threshold of that which is mysterious. This is an important factor, because it shows how much the human soul can and must make use of its extraordinary capacity to open up to the transcendent. Repressing this desire would be equivalent to impoverishing the richness of human nature, preventing it from best expressing its openness toward the infinite.

Faced with such a universal phenomenon, science seeks to identify the profound reasons behind it. The historian, for example, will seek out documents that show the extent of the pilgrimages recorded up until now. The sociologist, for his part, will try to identify the repercussions of such mass movements, while the psychologist will seek out the hidden motives which lead a person to undertake a sacred journey. The theologian, perhaps more naively, sees pilgrimage as a sign of faith and therefore seeks to understand the phenomenon from a broader perspective. He tries to grasp the widest possible significance of the event, combining faith with life and with the personal reflection that every human being undertakes deep within. The spiritual dimension and the anthropological dimension work together, rather than against each other, and this synthesis allows the pilgrim to experience pilgrimage in all its wonder, even in everyday life. In short, pilgrimage makes visible the profound truth of every human existence: that constant and dynamic growth, always open to and in search of fulfillment.

This indicates the true nature of mankind: *homo viator*! The root of the word *pilgrim* helps us see this. The word *Peregrinus*, in Latin, has two possible derivations: *per ager*, indicating the one who crosses fields; and *per eger*, meaning the one who crosses borders. In both cases, the pilgrim is a stranger, a foreigner, a person en route to a destination. This is what distinguishes the pilgrim from the wanderer, who has no goal in sight and wanders aimlessly without knowing what he is looking for.

Each of us is on a journey. Forgetting this would be the equivalent of ignoring the meaning and measure of our humanity and mean going round in circles with an illusion of immortality which would eventually lead us unconsciously to the grave. The truth is that we are always on a journey, wherever we are. For some this means seeking a path toward the truth; for others, the path is an anxious search for inner peace; and for others still, the path leads to an encounter with God. However it manifests itself, it is the sign of a profound, almost innate, need for a journey that helps us grasp the profound spirituality within us.

Jesus as companion on the journey

A scene described by the evangelist Luke can help us discover another essential element of Christian pilgrimage. Immediately after the death of Jesus, two disciples were walking from Jerusalem toward a village called Emmaus. They hadn't set out on a pilgrimage, but it quickly became one. They were chatting about events that had recently happened, the passion and death of their Master, and how their hopes for a Messiah had been dashed. At that moment Jesus himself approached them and started walking with them. The question he asked them seemed innocuous enough: "What are you discussing with each other as you walk along?" (Lk 24:17). The surprised response of the two disciples gives rise to one of the most significant exchanges in the history of the Church. The disciples' disappointment which can be sensed in the phrase "we had been hoping that he would be the one who would redeem Israel" (v. 21) is the opening which allows the risen Lord to revisit the whole of Sacred Scripture in the light of his presence: "'How foolish you are, and how slow to believe all that the Prophets have spoken! Was it not necessary that the Christ should suffer these things and enter into his glory?' Then, beginning with Moses and going through all the Prophets, he interpreted for them all the passages from the Scriptures that pertained to him" (vv. 26–27).

The three arrive at the inn and Christ breaks the bread as on the day of the Last Supper. Finally, "their eyes were opened and they recognized him" (v. 31). It is extremely significant to think that Christian pilgrimage begins with Jesus accompanying his disciples. This is the real pilgrimage of the Church, always called upon to discover the face of Christ in the central mystery of his life: the *Eucharist.* In a sense, Christians are called not to fix their gaze for too long on any place in this world, even the most sacred. They must be ready to meet Christ where he has made his permanent home. This home is in the mystery of his Eucharistic presence, where forever, and in a true and real way, he offers himself to those who believe in him as bread that leads to eternal life.

Perhaps it is for this reason that the angel rebukes the women who arrived as the first pilgrims at the tomb of Christ: "Why do you look among the dead for one who is alive? He is not here. He has been raised" (Lk 24:5). The great temptation of mankind is that of always wanting to set up a tent where he can be certain of finding God whenever he wants. We see this in the Scriptures when Jacob, forgetting quickly that he had lost a battle with God that had lasted all night, decides to build an altar in Bethel "because God had revealed himself there" (Gn 32:7). But he whom the highest heaven cannot contain, is he likely to stay in a house built by human hands? Wasn't this Jesus' point when he appealed to the Samaritan woman: "Believe me, woman, the hour is coming when you will worship the Father neither on this mountain nor in Jerusalem" (Jn 4:21)?

The gaze of Christians, therefore, must always be fixed on what is essential. The sign given to them is a powerful reminder of the ultimate meaning that it contains — namely, that the pilgrim's destination is the heavenly Jerusalem. This objective cannot be obscured by any sanctuary that would serve only to distract man's gaze from what is essential for our faith. Christ in the Eucharist strengthens us so that we may bring the good news of the Gospel to every creature.

The story of the disciples at Emmaus, however, can serve as a good starting point for understanding the value and meaning of Christian pilgrimage. It is a journey made in the company of the Risen One. Pilgrimage is never undertaken alone. Even when the pilgrim is physically alone, he brings his community with him and can never be separated from it. Indeed, pilgrimage is a path that brings the men and women of our time closer together; you ask questions, but you are also challenged to give answers.

We should set out with the curiosity of someone wanting to discover what lies in the human heart in order to be able to effectively communicate the message of salvation. The pilgrim, in this way, becomes a modern prophet. The words of the apostle Paul cannot leave anyone unmoved: "If everyone is prophesying and an unbeliever or uninstructed person should enter, he would be reproved by all and judged by all, and the secrets of his heart would be revealed. Then he would fall down and worship God, declaring, 'God is truly in your midst'" (1 Cor 14:24–25). Speaking heart to heart, therefore, is all about searching for the essential, and this is well understood by those who have lived their lives in a perennial, dynamic search for the truth.

Pilgrims along the paths of the earth

The favorite destination for pilgrims, certainly from the fourth century onward, was the Holy Land. This territory encapsulated their fascination with the mystery of the life of Jesus Christ and was seen as the natural destination for every Christian who wanted to return to the origins of his faith. There are various accounts relating to this pilgrimage. Saint Jerome is among the first to attest that many "bishops, martyrs, and doctors of the Church ...were convinced that they would have possessed less religiosity, less science, and less virtue if they had not adored Christ in the very places from which the Gospel had begun to radiate from the scaffold." From the first centuries, the pilgrimages of the bishops Alexander of Cappadocia and Melito of Sardis are remembered, but written testimonies are also found in the diaries of Egeria, a Spanish noblewoman who sometime in the 380s went as a pilgrim to the Holy Land, describing the journey's most important stages.

Even before that, however, just after the Edict of Milan (A.D. 313), a guide for pilgrims to the land of Jesus was in circulation. The historical events which involved wars for the conquest and liberation of the holy places are well known. The Crusades mark, in some ways, the culmination of this period, but they cannot be seen through a simplistic narrative based on ideological rather than historical evidence. In terms of the *phenomenon* of pilgrimage to the Holy Land, however, the fact remains that wars made the journey especially dangerous for pilgrims.

Faith and devotion later identified other, safer places which soon became the focus of great pilgrimages. The fall of Jerusalem into the hands of the Muslims in 638/640 brought the city of Rome, the "other Jerusalem," to the fore, and, along with Santiago de Compostela it became a major destination for pilgrimages. In the thirteenth century interest grew still further with the presence in the city of the "relic of Veronica." This true icon of Our Lord had become one of the most venerated images throughout the West, more important even than the tomb of the apostle in Compostela.

It is in this context that we should see the pilgrimages which were made for jubilees over the years to the tombs of Peter and Paul. The various papal bulls, with which Holy Years were announced, act as a common thread identifying the practices asked of the pilgrim. In *Antiquorum Habet*, which begins the history of the jubilees, Boniface VIII establishes that the *romei* — as pilgrims to Rome were then known — should visit St. Peter's Basilica to obtain an indulgence for their sins. Here are the provisions that the pope gave for the celebration of the first Jubilee:

> So that the most blessed apostles Peter and Paul will be honored all the more widely, the more devoutly their basilicas in the city will be frequented by the faithful, and the faithful themselves will feel more filled by the bestowal of spiritual gifts from visits of this kind, we, trusting in the mercy of almighty God and in the merits and authority of his apostles themselves, on the advice of our brothers, and in the fullness of apostolic power concede and grant to all those who, in the present year 1300 starting from the recently celebrated feast of the Nativity of our Lord Jesus Christ, and in every hundredth year that follows, go with reverence to the

> same basilicas truly repentant and having confessed, or that in the present hundredth year of this kind and in any hundredth year that follows they will truly repent and confess, receiving not only a full and extensive, but a very full forgiveness of all their sins. [For this reason] we establish that those who wish to participate in the indulgence of this kind granted by us, should go to the same basilicas, if they are Romans, for thirty continuous or occasional days at least once a day. If instead they are pilgrims or foreigners, they should do so in the same way for fifteen days. Everyone, however, will deserve more and will obtain the indulgence more effectively if they frequent the same basilicas more widely and more devoutly.

Later, a visit to the four major basilicas (St. Peter's, St. Paul Outside the Walls, St. Mary Major and St. John Lateran) became mandatory for the gaining of the indulgence. The Basilica of Santa Croce in Gerusalemme was later added to this list, and from time to time, the practice of pilgrimage was extended, giving it new significance. St. Philip Neri, for example, established the practice of visiting the seven churches, which remains to this day one of the best-known devotions of the Jubilee celebrations.

Even outside the context of Jubilee years, we cannot forget that millions of people make pilgrimages to the various sanctuaries around the world every year. The most popular Marian shrines, such as Lourdes, Fátima, and Guadalupe, welcome only a small percentage of that multitude every year. This surely shows how much the faith of believers needs places and times that remind them of the call to holiness of their baptism. It cannot be denied that this kind of popular devotion plays a huge role in the Christian life, a form of catechesis recalling the essentials of the faith. A catechesis, for example, aimed at understanding the real meaning of the Communion of Saints could help us understand the practice of pilgrimage, allowing us to discover the truth about devotion to the Virgin Mother of God and the saints.

Having almost completely lost its original penitential meaning, pilgrimage cannot, however, lapse into a mere form of religious tourism in which, for a good price, one can combine elements that are both useful and pleasant. When it is freed from superstition, simplified, and stripped of elements of mere folklore, and brought back to its original meaning, pilgrimage is a real vehicle of human and spiritual growth.

The awareness of one's condition as a human being on a perpetual journey, combined with faith in a goal to be strived for, are an encouragement to seek what is essential in life, without wasting one's days in an unbridled race toward goals which ultimately lead to disappointment. Pilgrimage, which involves *silence, prayer, penance*, and *charity*, remains even today, a worthy form of human living that cannot and should not be dismissed.

Pilgrims rejoicing in the beauties of nature, silently contemplating the sunrise or sunset, a starry sky or a mountaintop, or gazing at the masterpieces of art that faith has inspired … this should not just be a poetic vision. Modern man and woman can truly proclaim the beauty of creation with their pilgrimage, turning their mind to the Creator and singing of the glory due to him. In short, pilgrims can make their own the psalmist's prayer:

Praise the Lord from the heavens;
  offer praise to him in the heights!
Praise him, all his angels;
  offer praise to him, all his hosts!
Praise him, sun and moon;
  offer praise to him, all you shining stars!
Praise him, you highest heavens,
  and you waters above the heavens.

Let them praise the name of the Lord,
  for it was at his command that they were created.
He established them in place forever and ever;
  he issued a law that will never pass away.
Praise the Lord from the earth,
  you sea monsters and ocean depths,
fire and hail, snow and clouds,
  storm winds that carry out his word,
all mountains and hills,
  all fruit trees and cedars,
wild animals and all cattle,
  creeping creatures and flying birds,
kings of the earth and all nations,
  princes and all rulers on the earth,
young men and women,
  the elderly, as well as children.
Let them all praise the name of the Lord,
  for his name alone is exalted;
  his majesty is above the earth and the heavens.
He has raised high a horn for his people,
  to the glory of all his saints,
  for the people of Israel who are close to him.
(Psalm 148)

For modern man and woman, increasingly immersed in a high-tech culture, the need to get back to contact with nature and encounter others along the way is an urgent necessity. Pilgrimage can be an answer to this need and allows us to go deeper, beyond the superficial level of life at which we too often operate.

5
The Journey to Rome

Rome is not just any old city. It never has been, and it never will be. For good or ill it will remain a city that is unique in the world. It's not appropriate to compare it to other metropolises that are magnets for tourism. The uniqueness of Rome is far more than this. It is unique both because of its history and its vocation. A mysterious but very real design of providence has placed this city at the heart of the world. It is a crossroads for a series of worlds, from the arts to diplomacy, from culture to commerce, from politics to religion.

It bears within it the glories of the ancient empire and at the same time the degradation of a modern metropolis. Centuries of history have contrived to combine within it the ancient and the modern, the pagan and the Christian, without one overshadowing the other. Alas, this has not always gone well. Various monuments bear scars, which show the violence they have undergone over the years.

Yet Rome is not a city marked by signs of division. Instead, the grandeur of continuity emerges, allowing a visitor's gaze to fall more easily on the beauty of days of old, days sometimes forgotten, while hiding away some aspects of its present, especially the poverty of its outlying districts.

To obtain a rudimentary understanding of Rome's development, visitors should go to the Via dei Fori Imperiali. Halfway up, walking toward the Colosseum, we come across a very significant monument on the right. On the wall can be seen four plinths which tell the story of the city's development. In the first, Rome is represented by a white dot sitting solemnly amid the blackness of the surrounding space — this is the time of the city's foundation. By the fourth plinth we are looking at the extension of the empire in the time of Trajan — the golden era. The black stone gives way to white indicating the fullest expansion of the Roman empire. At this point Rome truly deserved to be called *caput mundi* ("capital of the world"). "*Contra factum non valent argumenta*," as the ancients would say — that is, loosely, "you can't argue with facts." This is the history of Rome!

But Rome means much more than just a history of empire. Some of the writings of Ambrose from the period of the end of the Roman empire help us see that the presence of Christianity in the city was not a question of luck, but rather a special vocation Rome knew how to embrace warmly. We should never forget, because it gave to the city the greatness which makes it unique in the world.

If, in the eyes of the world, Rome became great — *caput mundi* — because of its role as a crossroads, a meeting point, a place of welcome and shared living between different peoples, so much so that it became known as *mater gentium* e *communis patria* ("mother of peoples" and "common homeland"), the same special role was attributed to the city by her sister churches. It was to Rome that the title *omnium urbium et orbis ecclesiarum mater et caput* ("the mother and head of all churches in the city and the world") was granted, as the inscription on the front of the

Basilica of St. John Lateran reads.

Ignatius of Antioch could be said to speak for all the churches in a letter he wrote to the Christians of Rome at the end of the first century. He addressed them as follows:

> Ignatius, Theophorus, to her who has received mercy from the magnificence of the most high and from Jesus Christ his only Son, the Church loved and enlightened by the will of him who willed into existence all things, in the faith and charity of Jesus Christ our God, [the Church] which presides in the land of Rome, worthy of God, of veneration, of praise, of success, of candor, which presides in charity, which bears the law of Christ and the name of the Father. *(Introductory greeting, Letter to the Romans)*

The genetic code of Rome, therefore, is so special as to make this city unique and eternal. It is placed at the converging points of a universal message, so much so that popular parlance rightly says that "all roads lead to Rome."

Thinking of Rome as a city with a special vocation is not really such a far-fetched idea. Anyone examining its location quickly realizes it could not have aspired to be what it has become based solely on its geographical position. Nestled between two opposing bends of the River Tiber, Rome was once nothing more than a village perched on the Palatine Hill. From the Palatine, Rome, to quote the description of Raymond Oursel:

> Extended little by little toward the low-lying plains that flanked the river to the east, where, in the basin which like a wide corridor separates the Capitoline Hill and the Palatine Hill from the Esquiline, the Forum and the colossal Flavian Amphitheater later arose. It climbed the "seven

> hills," which gave it its specific imprint and its popularity, and in the end it absorbed them, so much so that the first circle of walls, erected at the time of King Servius Tullius, had to be replaced by Emperor Aurelian with a new set of walls which included the Aventine, the Caelian, the entire Esquiline, the Pincio, and extended onto the left bank of the Tiber until it touched the southern slope of the Janiculum. (*Vie di pellegrinaggi e santuari*)

It was from this new construction that the various consular roads opened up, which would connect Rome with the rest of the world. The Via Ostiense and the Via Portuense connected it with the two ports of Ostia and Traiano. The Via Traiana connected it with Bari and Brindisi, while the Via Salaria and the Via Flaminia opened access to the Adriatic Sea. Then there were the great communication arteries which allowed one to travel the length and breadth of the empire. First, the Via Appia, which led to the south of Italy, but which, linking up with the Via Aurelia, allowed the north to be reached by passing through Pisa and reaching Genoa. The Via Emilia channeled traffic coming from France and connected Piacenza with Bologna and Rimini, while the Via Claudia reached the Alps at the Brenner Pass. All these roads built by Rome to allow its legions to conquer the world were also the roads that made it wealthy through commerce. These roads were traveled by the apostles Peter and Paul and by the first Christians who evangelized the empire. And even before the fall of the empire, along these same roads, pilgrims walked toward Rome to pray at the tombs of the apostles and martyrs.

A Church of martyrs

In reality, Rome's vocation as a Christian city was born under the shadow of, and amid the glory of, the martyrs. To understand Rome, therefore, we must understand the value of martyrdom.

Martyrdom is not an appendix to the Christian life, but rather its culmination. The martyr lives out his full devotion to Christ and identifies with him in the offering of his earthly life to the Father. By totally renouncing his life, the martyr bears witness to the truth of the faith he professes and proclaims that there is nothing more precious than full and total love for Christ. The martyr, therefore, is a sign encouraging people to become more self-aware, to acknowledge fully the freedom they desire, and to realize that a person really can die for love.

The martyrs should not be strangers to us. We know who they are, can identify their personalities, and can acknowledge their historical significance, even if too often their image evokes in us a world which seems far from our own. In the West, especially where the testimony of faith seems to have become increasingly lazy, tired, and halfhearted, the call to martyrdom takes on a new urgency. The strength of the Eastern Churches, which until recently suffered prison, torture, and death for their fidelity as Christians, has in a way supported the increasingly diminished faith of the West, marked by years of carefree well-being.

Today we look around, almost in bewilderment, incapable even of imagining that devotion to the Christian faith might lead someone to death. For many of us, Christian faith is not much more than a simple weekly pious practice. Inevitably, faith in many Western countries has entered a period of profound crisis. It is no coincidence that the West feels the need for a new evangelization to recover the enthusiasm of a weak and often dormant faith.

The West itself, however, also needs martyrs. This is said not out of cynicism or from a distorted viewpoint, but rather to raise a vital question about the intensity of Christian living and the future of the Church itself. The martyr is the one who speaks through actions. His word is his life, and his death is the supreme choice of freedom. He is the only one who allows us to understand the beauty of Christian dying, the one who does not give up, and the one who knows how to love right to the end. This allows us to compare the martyr with the person of Jesus Christ who, out of love, offers his life in obedience to the saving will of the Father (cf. Jn 3:16; 10:17–18). When faced with the figure of the martyr, we cannot put his or her faith down either to chance or fortuitous circumstances. In the martyr we encounter a person who has made a conscious, clear, and lucid choice: knowing that the disciple is no more than his Master and that if they have persecuted the Master, they will also persecute those who believe in him. Without this awareness, faith will never reach maturity. For this reason, no one who has seriously considered being a Christian can think that martyrdom is not for him.

The martyr's story runs through the history of the Church which, even before becoming a "Church of martyrs," was by its very nature a martyr Church insofar as it is the body of the only true martyr. Perhaps an unavoidable question arises: Is it still possible to be a martyr in a period such as ours, in which indifference reigns supreme? The answer is provided with great clarity in a quote from John Paul II's *Tertio Millennio Adveniente*: "At the end of the second millennium, the Church has once again become a Church of martyrs. The persecutions against believers —priests, religious, and lay people — have caused a great sowing of martyrdom in various parts of the world" (37). It seems strange to think that in the era of greatest freedom there can still be martyrs; yet that is reality. The Church of our time is still, fortunately, watered by their blood. Even in our own days, which seem so far from the barbarism of the first centuries, martyrs exist, because the rejection of Christ and his Gospel continues. By the grace of God, to this day the Church can count on their testimony and see the spread of the Gospel through the shedding of their blood. The words of Tertullian in the second century, according to which "the blood of Christians is a seed" that allows the growth and spread of the Faith, remain as true today as they ever were.

Over the years, strong ideological pressures have tried to dismiss the value of martyrdom. It is no coincidence that the Church's critics have tried to undermine the martyrs' credibility. Intent on destroying any foundation for the Faith, they focus on the one thing which, above all, can be used to contradict their arguments. In their crazy logic they see the martyr as the true enemy, for the simple reason that the martyr is a coherent witness to the truth. One only has to reread certain pages of some modern authors and philosophers to see this drama playing out. They echo in the abyss into which Friedrich Nietzsche's words fell: "Their madness taught that the truth must be demonstrated through the shedding of their blood. But blood is the worst witness to the truth; blood poisons even the purest doctrine and silent madness and sows hatred in man's heart."

We cannot help but perceive in these words a certain degree of envy on the part of those who do not know how to love, and who do not understand the truth of the gift of pure selflessness. If we focus on the contemporary world, trying to understand its actions, the anxieties and hopes that fill it, it becomes clear why the witness of the martyrs is a testimony not to be forgotten. By God's grace we can recognize the faces of new martyrs who did not flee from death for the sake of the Gospel and out of loyalty to the Church.

Paradoxical as it may seem, the martyrs are our contemporaries. Young people, boys and girls, men and women of all ages, are still killed, raped, tortured, mocked, and marginalized just because they are Christians. How many names could fill a new and updated martyrology of our own age! Unfortunately, the twentieth century saw a greater number of Christian martyrs than the nineteen centuries that preceded it. The transition into the twenty-first century, sadly, is lengthening the list without any sign of a decrease or even a pause. What makes this situation so hard to grasp is the silence of so many people who have become complicit in our apparent inability to eradicate violence.

Re-presenting the martyrs today, with a renewed energy, is not the same as idealizing their actions or seeing them in the context of heroism. Martyrdom, on the contrary, is so close to everyday life and to people's sentiments that it is the best expression of the *simplicity* of the Christian life. Its great strength lies in its unshakable certainty that faith must be taken seriously, and that the truth of the Christian message really does have a definitive meaning for every human being. It also underlines the fact that, even today, it is worth running the risk of violence, rather than giving up on love, which is surely the only thing that really transforms individual lives and the life of society. As we contemplate the figure of the martyr, therefore, there is no room for rhetoric. The blood they shed reminds us of how to personally assume responsibility for the faith.

As the papal bull for the Jubilee states:

> The most convincing testimony to this hope is provided by the martyrs. Steadfast in their faith in the Risen Christ, they renounced life itself here below, rather than betray their Lord. Martyrs, as confessors of the life that knows no end, are present and numerous in every age, and perhaps even more so in our own day. We need to treasure their testimony, in order to confirm our hope and allow it to bear good fruit. The martyrs, coming as they do from different Christian traditions, are also seeds of unity, expressions of the ecumenism of blood. (*Spes Non Confundit*, 20)

The hope we need, therefore, also comes through their testimony of confident abandonment to the Father's love.

An image from the Book of the Apocalypse offers a fitting conclusion to this brief reflection on the value of martyrdom in our day:

> One of the elders spoke to me and inquired, "Who are these people, all dressed in white robes, and where have they come from?" I replied, "My lord, you are the one who knows." Then he said to me, "These are the ones who have survived the great tribulation. They have washed their robes and made them white in the blood of the Lamb." (Revelation 7:13–14)

The blood they shed does not stain the body; on the contrary, it makes it clean and pure, ready for the definitive baptism of communion with the Risen One. It is not the one who speaks who has the most impact — for words can soon descend into idle chatter — but the one who acts. Or, to put it another way, the one who makes his word a concrete testimony of his life. This is the person chosen to become a martyr. People are afraid of such individuals, because their life becomes like a light which shines on and exposes both the inconsistency of our own actions and the emptiness of our words. The big issues of life, therefore, are at stake here, knowing that the meaning of existence lies elsewhere. The martyr affirms by his actions the truth of his love for Christ. Reflecting on the martyr's choice, we, too, are challenged to reiterate that "no one can have greater love than to lay down his life for his friends" (Jn 15:13).

City of Peter and Paul

Christian Rome is first and foremost the city where Peter and Paul bore witness to Christ with their lives. The words of Pope Leo the Great come to mind, when, in his sermon written about the year 440 for the feast of Saints Peter and Paul, he said:

> Today's feast, besides the veneration which echoes around the whole world, should be celebrated with a special joy in our city, so that in the very place where the glorious death of the Princes of the Apostles took place, there might be found the greatest joy on the day of their martyrdom. Rome, remember that these are the men who caused the light of the Gospel of Christ to shine before you, making of you a disciple of truth. These are your holy fathers and true pastors who, linking you to the kingdom of heaven, established you much better and more happily than did those who laid the foundation stones of your walls. These are the ones who raised you to such glory as a holy nation, a chosen people, a royal and priestly city, which has become the capital of the world because Peter established his see here.

This presence, therefore, is indelible and animates the life of the Church in Rome, a Church which can never forget those who founded it and the price they paid. The first persecution recorded was that of Nero. It was in the year A.D. 64 that the apostle Peter was taken away to be martyred. Three years later it fell to Paul, the missionary Apostle of the Gentiles, to give his powerful witness to Christ by being decapitated. Right from the beginning, therefore, the Church has celebrated the feast of these two apostles, uniting them in the same hymn of praise for the unique testimony of their martyrdom. (The date of June 29 for the feast of Saints Peter and Paul was chosen as far back as the year 258.) Soon further persecutions were to follow. In the year 250, Emperor Decius launched a particularly bloody persecution, and no less violent were those which followed under Emperors Valerian (257) and Diocletian (310).

One text, dating back to the earliest days of Christianity, serves as a dependable source in describing the sufferings of the martyrs. The text in question is known as the Martyrdom of Polycarp and was written in the year 155. It is the careful and accurate description, without any hint of polemics or apologetics, of how Polycarp, the bishop of Smyrna, was martyred at the age of 86. The information it contains helps us understand the cruelty also perpetrated on eleven other men who died alongside their bishop simply for being Christians:

> Who could fail to be amazed at their generosity of spirit, their patience, and their love of God? Their flesh torn open by flagellation, so much so that the internal anatomy of their bodies with the veins and arteries was visible to the naked eye. They remained steadfast even while onlookers were moved to tears by their suffering. These men had such strength that not one of them cried out, showing everyone that in the moment of their supreme suffering when they were being put to the test, these generous martyrs for Christ seemed not to be living in their own bodies. It was as if the Lord was standing next to them, talking to them. ... In the same way those who were condemned to be thrown to wild beasts underwent horrific torments, stretched out on shells, and slashed using other forms of torture designed to make them abjure their faith. (*Martyrdom of Polycarp*)

One of the first things the Christians did, when allowed to do so, was to collect the remains of the martyrs and place them in a *martyrion* (tomb). They would go to visit these sites, almost as if on a pilgrimage *ante litteram* to pray and celebrate the *dies natalis* of the martyr. The *Martyrdom of Polycarp* provides us with this information:

> He took steps to ensure that Polycarp's body was not taken from us, although many wanted to do so, so as to possess a fragment of his holy flesh. He suggested to Nicetas, the father of Herod the police chief, brother of Alce, to go to the governor asking him not to hand over the remains. Leaving the crucified one aside — he said — they will begin to venerate the martyr. … They didn't realize that we can never abandon Christ who suffered innocently for sinners, for the salvation of those who are redeemed throughout the whole world, to worship another. We venerate him who is the Son of God, and we worthily honor the martyrs as disciples and imitators of the Lord for their immense love for their king and master. … The centurion, having listened to the reasoning of the Jews, placed the remains in the middle and had them burned as was the custom. We later collected his bones, more precious than expensive gems and more esteemed than gold and placed them in a more convenient place. As soon as possible, gathering there in serenity and joy, the Lord will allow us to celebrate the birthday into heaven of the martyr, a reminder of those who fought before and an encouragement to those who have still to fight.

From these few details we can understand the love that the Church has always reserved for its martyrs, and rightly so. This explains why Rome, as early as the fourth century, felt the need to regulate the cult of martyrs and visits to their tombs. Thanks to the recognition received from Constantine, the Church of Rome began to build great basilicas. On Peter's tomb, the emperor himself decided that there should be a large church. Its construction was to last 25 years and would be completed in 337, becoming, from that day onward, a powerful reference point for

Christians throughout the world. Work also began on the site of Paul's tomb, on the road that leads to Ostia. The large basilica, which has been rebuilt several times, was to indicate the place where the apostle who had become "all things to all men" gave to Christ the final proof of his love.

The graffiti discovered over the years near these sites not only indicate the names of the pilgrims who visited the tombs of the apostles from far and near, but, more importantly, show the prayers that were addressed to the martyrs. It turns out that, unlike our prayer, the first Christians never asked to be freed from illness or present suffering, but rather focused on intercession for their life after death. "Peter and Paul I recommend to you the soul of Chalcedon": This inscription from the third century summarizes the prayer of the early pilgrim.

Visits to the catacombs and to the tombs of Peter and Paul, therefore, were at the heart of pilgrimages for the first Jubilee of 1300. Thereafter, Rome increasingly became a destination for pilgrimages, especially when there was the opportunity to gain the "great indulgence." At first, this happened every 100 years, then 50, then 33, and, finally, every 25 years. The gift of the indulgence, however, was always subject to undertaking a pilgrimage to Peter's tomb.

It would be unfair, in this context, to forget another special place of prayer and pilgrimage: the basilica of St. Mary Major (*Santa Maria Maggiore*). This was the first sanctuary in the city, and in the world, dedicated to the Virgin Mother of God. An ancient tradition tells us that on the night of August 5, 352, an unusual phenomenon revealed the divine will. On that summer night, the Virgin Mary appeared in a dream to Pope Liberius, and to a married couple, asking them to build a church in her honor in the place where it had snowed that night. Snow on the Esquiline Hill in a Roman August! The shrine of Mary was indeed built, and one of the first names given to the basilica was

Our Lady of Snows (*Santa Maria ad nives*). It seemed right that alongside the cult of martyrs there should also be a basilica dedicated to the Queen of Martyrs (*Regina martyrum*). It was only a few years earlier, in 341, that a council had been convened in Ephesus which had proclaimed Mary *Theotokos* — literally, "house of God" — indicating that she was the true Mother of God, of that Son who was made flesh for the salvation of all mankind.

The next Jubilee will see new pilgrim routes opened in Rome to give pilgrims the opportunity to undertake new spiritual journeys. *Spes Non Confundit* says:

> In Rome itself, along with the usual visits to the catacombs and the Seven Churches, other itineraries of faith will be proposed. … The Jubilee churches along the pilgrimage routes and in the city of Rome can serve as oases of spirituality and places of rest on the pilgrimage of faith, where we can drink from the wellsprings of hope, above all by approaching the Sacrament of Reconciliation, the essential starting point of any true journey of conversion. In the particular churches, special care should be taken to prepare priests and the faithful to celebrate … confession and to make it readily available in its individual form. (5)

The 2025 pilgrim will be able to walk along the *Iter Europaeum*, which consists of the twenty-seven churches that have a link to the member states of the European Union. The church of the *Ara coeli* also plays a special role, recalling the signing of the Treaties of Rome at the nearby Roman Campidoglio on March 25, 1957, which served as a kind of "birth certificate" for the European Union. Another pilgrim route will help people appreciate the role of the female patrons of Europe and female Doctors of the Church. This symbolic journey will allow pilgrims to discover places often not quoted in official itineraries, but which are nonetheless rich in history and spirituality.

The See of Peter's successor

The uniqueness of Rome has another essential characteristic: the see of the successor of Peter. It is no coincidence that the period in which the popes moved to Avignon was also the most decadent period in the history of Rome. A visit to the city, therefore, cannot fail to consider the figure of the pope and the importance it has for the life and faith of the Church. A good starting point for this topic appears at the end of the Gospel of John. This text reveals how much the Christian community already recognized the unique ministry that had been entrusted to Peter by the Lord:

> After this, he said to him, "Follow me." Peter looked around and saw the disciple whom Jesus loved following them — the one who had reclined next to Jesus at the supper and had asked, "Lord, who is it that will betray you?" When Peter saw him, he said to Jesus, "Lord, what about him?" Jesus replied, "If it should be my will that he remains until I come, how does that concern you? Follow me!" (21:19–22)

So twice, in a few verses, Jesus says to Peter, "Follow me." Even when Peter gets distracted by thinking "not as God does, but as men do" (Mt 16:23), he is reminded that his primary mission is to follow the Master. It is within the context of this following of Jesus that Peter's whole life can be viewed, from his first calling until the day of his supreme testimony to Christ. Mark recalls this with few but precise words: "Walking along by the Sea of Galilee, he saw Simon and his brother Andrew casting their nets into the sea, for they were fishermen. Jesus said to them, "Come, follow me" (Mk 1:16–17). Peter himself recalls this moment when he tries to provoke the Master into giving an answer that satisfies him: "We have given up everything to follow you" (Mt 19:27).

But the following of the Lord must respect the times established by the Father: "Jesus answered, 'Where I am going you cannot follow me now; but you will follow me later" (Jn 13:36). Peter, at this moment, represents the idea that following Christ is the primary choice every believer who comes to faith must make. Without this command to follow Jesus, little would be understood about Peter, and nothing about the Christian faith. One would easily fall into mere sociological analyzes or specious ideological readings, depriving faith of its uniqueness and misunderstanding its content.

The figure of the apostle and his ministry has a clear foundation in the teaching of Sacred Scripture and of the Church Fathers. His importance is not accidental. The evangelist Mark, who is always sparse in his information, is nevertheless precise and meticulous when he speaks about Peter. From the sacred texts emerges a generous and at the same time fearful, enthusiastic, and sometimes insecure character. He is one of those deeply human individuals with whom each of us can identify. He is the only one to have his name changed by Jesus (cf. Mk 3:16). On behalf of the Twelve, it is he who makes the first profession of faith in the Lord by recognizing him as the Messiah (Mk 8:29–30). It is he who challenges the Master by asking him to join him walking on the water, and it is fear that pushes him to call for Jesus' help (Mt 14:28–30). Jesus entrusts Peter with the keys of his kingdom and with the power to bind and loose (Mt 16:18–19), in order to build his Church. He will be the first to realize, albeit with fear, that the Word is destined to spread beyond the narrow borders of Israel as recounted in Acts 10.

Peter's primacy among the Twelve is beyond doubt. He is

chosen by the Master so that he can lead his Church and feed the flock entrusted to him. For this to happen, he is asked to follow the Lord. His fate and destiny is to do so radically, right to the end (cf. Jn 21:15–19). Peter's humanity, in a word, is a key part of the project of salvation and plays an indispensable role therein. To use von Balthasar's happy expression, he belongs to the "constellation" of Jesus of Nazareth.

The postapostolic Church never doubted Peter's primacy and his role within the Twelve. What is important to note is the fact that the Church of Rome, due to the recognized presence in it of Peter and Paul, and above all because they suffered martyrdom there, is considered the first of all the churches. It is the one which presides in charity, entrusted with the task of keeping the profession of faith in the Lord intact and pure. The Church that heard Peter's last sermon and witnessed his martyrdom thus acquires a unique place among the other churches.

Some of the writings of the Church Fathers strengthen still further the conviction expressed by the sacred texts. Ignatius, bishop of Antioch, a Church which itself enjoyed particular prestige for having been founded by Peter, addressed Rome as the Church which "presides in charity." Clement, bishop of Rome, writing in the year 95, spoke out against the Church of Corinth admonishing its Christians to reestablish peace and communion. Irenaeus, bishop of Lyons, in his *Adversus haereses* (*Against Heresies*), written in 180, used these words:

> To this Church of Rome, due to its most excellent origin, every Church must come, that is, those who are faithful; in it, the tradition that comes from the apostles has always been preserved for all men. The blessed apostles, after having founded and built the Church, handed over its episcopal administration to Linus, whom Paul mentions in his letters to Timothy. He was succeeded by

> Cletus. After him, in third place after the apostles, the episcopacy fell to Clement, who had also seen the apostles and spoken with them: He still had their preaching ringing in his ears and their tradition before his eyes; but he was not the only one, because many people were still alive who had been taught by the apostles. Under Clement, a significant disagreement occurred among the brothers who were in Corinth. The Church of Rome sent an important letter to the Corinthians, to lead them back to peace, to secure their faith and proclaim the tradition recently received from the apostles.

Many other texts could be cited, but those already quoted clearly indicate how the bishop of Rome carried out a particular service toward the other churches by virtue of his being the successor of Peter. The word *primate/primacy*, which is usually used to indicate the pope's ministry, was used for the first time at the Council of Nicaea. What emerges in the fourth century is of huge importance because it allows us to see the unanimity of the churches in believing that Rome preserved the Faith intact and without heresies and, therefore, its tradition could be considered the criterion for the true Faith.

In his book *A Commentary on the Apostles' Creed*, Rufinus (345–410) attests to this: "I think it is not out of place to recall that in various churches we find that things have been added to the words [of the Apostles' Creed]. However, this has not happened in the Church of Rome, I believe, because no heresy originated there, and the old tradition is preserved there so that those who are about to receive the grace of baptism repeat the creed publicly." This helps us to understand why, even though the three churches of Antioch, Alexandria, and Rome already had a primacy over all other churches, Rome held the position of absolute primacy above the other two. This does not mean that the bishop of Rome was recognized as having a different ministry from other bishops. But what does seem to emerge up to this point though is the priority given to the Church of Rome. But, one wonders, is it possible to conceive of a church without its bishop? Perhaps the most eloquent expression of this conviction is found in the formula of the Council of Chalcedon: "Peter spoke through the mouth of Leo."

From this panoply of facts, a question arises: What did Peter's faith consist of? Answering this question means, first, retracing 2,000 years of Church history. The Second Vatican Council provides a synthesis of this, and a key to understanding the conciliar teaching can be found in the following expression: "This college, insofar as it is composed of many, expresses the variety and universality of the People of God, but insofar as it is assembled under one head, it expresses the unity of the flock of Christ" (*Lumen Gentium*, 22). The fundamental themes that, theologically and pastorally, affect the pope can be traced back to this text: his ministry toward the entire Church, the primacy of the bishop of Rome, and his relationship with the College of Bishops.

In the ministry of Peter and, together with him, that of the bishops, the Church sees the sign of its call to universality in unity and communion in plurality. It is easier to understand the pope's mission if we condense it into a few key expressions. His first task is to feed the flock of Christ, by virtue of the supreme love that he owes to the Master (cf. Jn 21:15–17). Shepherding indicates an all-encompassing activity that is divided into different phases in which the ministry is made explicit. The pope has to "confirm" his brothers in the Faith and lead everyone to encounter the Lord in the faith that has always been professed by all believers in all places. At the same time, shepherding must also involve protecting and defending the flock. The pope's is a voice that is raised against any lack of respect for the dignity of the human person wherever these rights are offended or disregarded. It also cries out against war and injustice in all its forms. He is called to defend the flock against anyone who would try to destroy it, and he does so because he is not a mercenary, but a shepherd.

Another characteristic of the pope's ministry is that of vigilance. Since faith is embodied in history by individual human beings, it will always be subject to the historical dynamic of fidelity to the past, interpretation of the present, and anticipation and creativity for the future. This typical dynamic of the Christian faith exists, however, under a sword of Damocles. The history of the Church reveals how many errors have infiltrated the interpretation of her faith and life. Like Peter, his successor must assume the role of the prophet acting as a vigilant sentinel until morning comes (cf. Ez 3:17). A letter from Pope Leo I puts it like this: "If we do not intervene with the vigilance that is due to us, we would not be able to apologize to him who wanted us to be like sentinels."

The successor of Peter must, therefore, warn people, in season and out of season, about their responsibility to keep the Deposit of Faith safe, united to its source and intact. He must do this in every way possible, urging them on with love, teaching with courage, and commanding authoritatively. For this reason, he is Peter — that is, a strong rock capable of resisting any bad weather that may strike the house, because he is rooted and founded on the person of Jesus Christ, the center of faith (cf. Mt 7:24–25).

The successor of Peter also carries out the ministry of unity, of which he is also a sign. To be a sign of unity means acting in ways that remind people of the ultimate meaning of that word. The vocation of being "one flock, one shepherd" (cf. Jn 10:16) implies that the successor of Peter should work energetically to try to overcome divisions which persist. He should also strive to convince everyone — first his brothers in the one baptism, then those who believe in the one God, and by extension all those who sincerely seek the truth — that unity is not just a desire but something that can become a reality. John Paul II clearly expressed this service of unity in his encyclical *Ut Unum Sint.* Being a sign of unity implies, at the same time, becoming an instrument of discernment. The pope, since he is called to love more and therefore to practice forgiveness more, must be the first to bow low to wash and kiss the feet of his brethren. There is a circularity between faith and love, truth and charity that can never be broken.

As bishop of the Church of Rome, and by vocation the first witness of charity, the pope must be a sign of that love expressed in communion. Unity is founded in communion when it is lived in love. This means that the pope is recognized in every part of the world as the one who holds the primacy of love which "bears all things, believes all things, hopes all things, endures all things" (1 Cor 13:7). If he was able to speak all the languages of men, if he could give a teaching full of wisdom and truth, if he could distribute all the riches of the earth to the poor and had a faith that could move mountains, but was without that love that he promised to give to the Master more than all the others, he would only be a "noisy gong or a clanging cymbal" and "achieve nothing" (cf. 1 Cor 13:1–3).

Peter's ministry, in a word, is intimately connected with that of John. A scene from the Gospel of John helps us see the profound unity that binds Peter and John. The former is called to follow the Master, but he will have to do it in the manner of the latter — that is, by giving everything. Only love, in fact, will remain until the Lord returns as the most credible and convincing form of faith (cf. Jn 21:23).

Whoever sits on the chair of Peter will always have in mind that this cathedra was set up by the shedding of blood for Christ. Jesus wanted his future to be clear to Peter: To follow the Master would involve the same fate of misunderstanding, slander, violence, and death. The supreme call requires the total gift of self, which is expressed in martyrdom, a sign of the one to whom much was given because he loved much (cf. Jn 21:18–19).

In a period like our own, which is impressed by honors and privileges, it is timely to recall a ceremony which formed part of the coronation liturgy of the pope up until the time of Pope Paul VI. At a certain point in the proceedings, a cardinal would attract the pontiff's attention, holding up to him a ball of flax which was then set on fire while these words were recited: *Pater sancte, sic transit Gloria mundi* ("Holy Father, thus passes the glory of the world"). In an instant it was burnt and gone.

The ministry of Peter and his successors is not primarily that of being the "prince" of the apostles, as we read on the inscription above the entrance to St. Peter's Basilica. Rather, his ministry is better expressed in the words *servus servorum Dei* ("servant of the servants of God"), which is clearly a title more suited to the fisherman of Galilee. His existence is lived out in the privileged light of martyrdom. This is the road indicated to Peter by Jesus himself: he must always love more (cf. Jn 21:15–17).

6
The Holy Door

Christ is the door

"*Aperite mihi portam iustitiae*" ("Open to me the door of justice"). The sound of the hammer striking the Holy Door will symbolize the pope's request on December 24, 2024, Christmas Eve. This will be the real opening of the Ordinary Jubilee of 2025. The pope will be the first to pass through the Holy Door, will kiss the door frame, and will make his profession of faith. Almost ten years after the last (extraordinary) Jubilee of Mercy called by Pope Francis for 2016, the same door will be opened to welcome all those who come as pilgrims to invoke the mercy and forgiveness of the Father.

From the documents in our possession, we know that during the first Jubilee in history pilgrims — *romei*, as they were known — did not pass through any door. The papal bull *Antiquorum Habet* makes no reference to doors, nor is there any reference to doors in the instructions given to pilgrims to obtain the indulgence. The first explicit reference to the Holy Door comes in the Jubilee of 1423, though, if truth be told, it appears that from the second Jubilee onward there was a custom of walking through a Holy Door. The door in question was always that of the Basilica of St. John Lateran, however; the lack of documentation on this subject means a variety of theories exist.

The image of the door holds extraordinary symbolic power. Various scriptural texts refer to a door as allowing access to one of the fundamental tenets of the faith — namely, the revelation of God in Jesus Christ. A glance at a few pages of the Bible can help us understand the meaning and value the sacred texts give to the door and its significance for the life of faith.

The first text which deserves our attention, because of the use that is made of it, is Psalm 118. As the pope strikes the Holy Door, he says aloud: "Open to me the door of justice." Psalm 118, written to celebrate the goodness and mercy of God, speaks of his constant closeness to his children, despite the many difficulties of life. The psalmist writes that God frees his faithful from danger and death and allows them to triumph over their enemies:

> In my distress I called out to the Lord;
>   he answered by setting me free.
> With the Lord to protect me I am not afraid.
>   What can mortals do to me?
> The Lord is at my side to offer me help;
>   I will look down upon my enemies.
> All the nations surrounded me;
>   in the name of the Lord I overcame them.
>
> (vv. 5–7, 10)

The New Testament offers us an even more profound key to understand this psalm. The words of verse 22, "The stone which the builders rejected / has become the cornerstone," were used by the early Christian communities who understood that the

Church, the new people of God, was built upon the rejected figure of Christ. Peter, in his first sermon, also uses this image, saying: "This is 'the stone rejected by you, the builders, / that has become the cornerstone.' There is no salvation in anyone else, nor is there any other name under heaven given to men by which we can be saved" (Acts 4:11–12).

The image of the door is used in reference to Christ, but also to the Church. In the hymns of Ephrem the Syrian there is a commentary on this text: "Blessed are the doors which are fully opened, your halls thrown open so that we can all find rest there." Christ shows us to the entrance of the house that will become a place of welcome for all peoples. Not everyone, however, can enter through that door. If we go back to the origins of the psalm we can understand why. It is easy to think of this psalm being chanted in procession as people approached the Temple in Jerusalem. As they arrived at the door, they would ask for admission: "Open for me the door of justice: I will enter and give thanks to the Lord." At this point, though, the priestly custodians of the Temple place conditions on the people's entry: "This is the gate of the Lord, / through which the righteous enter" (v 20). Entry to the Lord's temple, therefore, requires purification of heart and a commitment to a holy and coherent lifestyle.

The New Testament contains a fundamental passage linked to the symbolism of the door. The evangelist John refers to it in his Gospel. Jesus, speaking of the good shepherd who cares for his flock, affirms, "I am the gate of the sheepfold" (Jn 10:7). This phrase is worth examining further. The context in which it arises is the allegory of the sheep who recognize their shepherd's voice, and while the shepherd enters the sheepfold through the gate, the one who enters by another way is a "thief and a bandit" (v. 1). The reference to the door is first and foremost a reference to the shepherd's legitimacy — he is the one who has the right to enter the sheepfold because he knows the sheep "by name." Therefore, they belong to him, and his relationship with them is unique and unmistakable.

The identification of Christ with the door should be understood in this context. Various experts have offered different interpretations, but to really understand the teaching one has to grasp the full context of the discourse in which the image of the door has its own particular significance. What one notices immediately is the recognition of Christ as being the one who authentically reveals the Father, and thus is the only savior. The absoluteness of Jesus here eliminates any competitor. Others who, in the past or at that time, put forward a claim to be the savior of mankind see their claims collapse when faced with the real shepherd. The path of revelation, which ultimately leads to knowledge of the paternal face of God, can come about only through Jesus. It is for this reason that he is "the door." The sheep have only one way in, and that is through the person of Christ. So, there is only one bearer of salvation — Jesus Christ. He is the path we need to follow to reach the Father: "You know the way to the place I am going. I am the way, and the truth, and the life" (Jn 14:4, 6).

So, the path to salvation is indicated by Christ, who is the door giving access to the Father for the sheep searching for the meaning of life. As the one who reveals the Father, and as Son of God, he can make this claim. At the same time, he also becomes the criterion of truth, and therefore also of judgment and discernment, for those who want to fully understand the mystery. Therefore, if the sheep want to be safe and be able to reach safe pastures, they know whom they must follow. Only he whom the Father has sent can enter through this door, and only he can call them by their name.

A further insight into the meaning of the door is found in one of the oldest examples of Christian literature, the *Letter to the Corinthians* of Pope Clement, written about A.D. 95–98, which almost seems to have been written as a commentary on these texts:

> This is the door of justice open to life, as it is written: "Open for me the door of justice; I shall enter and call out the Lord's name. This is the door of the Lord, the just will enter through it." Many doors are opened, but the door of justice is in Christ. Blessed are all those who enter in and set their footsteps on the path of holiness and justice with great tranquility. Let each one be faithful, able to expound knowledge, let each one be wise in judging motives and pure in activities. It is even more important for a person to be humble if he is considered to be great, and he must always work for the common good and not his own ends. (Chapter 48)

Entering the Church

Going through the Holy Door we enter the St. Peter's Basilica, the sanctuary which houses the tomb and the relics of the apostle Jesus chose as head of his Church: "You are Peter, and on this rock I will build my Church" (Mt 16:18). This Gospel text is written in block capitals high around the apse of the basilica to remind those who enter both who the apostle was and the mission of his successors.

Before arriving at the Altar of the Confession, or high altar where the tomb of the apostle is found, the pilgrim will come to a bronze statue of Saint Peter on the right-hand side. The right foot of the statue is worn away by the touches and kisses of millions of pilgrims. These signs of devotion are not addressed to the statue itself, but indicate the affection and loyalty due to the successor of Peter. Since the excavations ordered by Pius XII in the 1950s, there is no longer any doubt that after his death Peter's body was placed under the high altar. Similarly, no one doubts the declaration of faith in Christ made by the first of the apostles. Clement records it faithfully some years later: "Because of unjust jealousy, [Peter] underwent not one or two, but many sufferings, and through his martyrdom reached the place of glory" (*Letter to the Corinthians,* Chapter 5).

As has already been noted, Emperor Constantine began work on the construction of the first basilica in 336. But it was mainly Michelangelo and Bernini who gave suitable glory to the tomb of the first of the apostles with works we can still admire today. Michelangelo's idea was that the tomb of Peter should be at the center of the basilica. All the geometric lines were to converge on that spot. But it is the great cupola, more than anything else, which highlights the heart of the Church. Bernini used his creative genius to crown the tomb with the solemn baldacchino, or canopy, which stands over the papal altar. Everything here seems to speak of faith — even the stones. Christians coming here quickly recognize it as something extraordinary and find the strength to make the same profession of faith for which Peter gave his life: "You are the Christ, the Son of the living God" (Mt 16:16).

All the artistic treasures and rich decoration of St. Peter's remind us that this temple has been rendered grandiose by art because of faith, and because of the significance of this building in the Christian life. The believer sees in this sacred building an image of the Church and believes firmly that the stones used to build God's dwelling place are a symbol of every baptized person who participates in the building of the kingdom of God on earth. It is Saint Peter himself who helps bring us to this realization. In his first letter he writes: "Come to him, a living stone, rejected by men but chosen by God and precious. You, too, are like living stones, being built up into a spiritual temple and a holy priesthood to offer spiritual sacrifices acceptable to God through Jesus Christ" (1 Pt 2:4–5).

The identification of Jesus as the living stone, the cornerstone on which the Church is built, is also present in the Gospels. In the parable of the tenants, the first Christian community immediately understood that Jesus was "the stone that the builders rejected" (Mk 12:9). The vine tenders plotted to take control of the vineyard by killing the son, the heir, but the designs of men are not the designs of God. His "thoughts are not your thoughts" (Is 55:8), and he has placed Christ as the cornerstone on which everything is based and on which everything will be built.

Jesus himself, had said as much to his disciples: "I will build my Church" (Mt 16:18). Paul, too, returns repeatedly to the image of construction when talking of the Church. In the Letter to the Ephesians he writes:

> As a result, you are no longer strangers and foreigners. Rather, you are fellow citizens of the saints and members of the household of God, built upon the foundation of the apostles and prophets, with Christ Jesus himself as the cornerstone. Through him the entire structure is joined together and grows into a holy temple in the Lord. In him you are also being built together into a dwelling place for God in the Spirit. (2:19–22)

These are rousing words, but they speak of a serious responsibility for the baptized, since they are addressed to them and require their serious commitment. As the community grows, the temptation grows also of thinking that everything is their own work, forgetting the importance of the foundations. But the Church is not a human society; rather, it is the presence of the Spirit who calls us to himself to make us members of the family of God. Forgetting this leads to the conclusion that "we" are the Church. If this is the understanding, divisions will surely follow. It is Paul who offers the following reflection:

> What then is Apollos? What is Paul? We are only servants through whom you have come to believe, as the Lord assigned each to accomplish. I planted the seed, and Apollos watered it, but God caused it to grow. Therefore, neither the one who plants nor the one who waters is of any importance but only God who causes the growth. The one who plants and the one who waters have a common end, and each will be rewarded in accordance with his labor. For we are God's coworkers; you are God's field, God's building. By the grace that God has given to me, I laid a foundation like a skilled master builder, and someone else is building on that foundation. But each one must be careful how he builds on it. For no one can lay any foundation other than the one that has already been laid, namely, Jesus Christ. (1 Corinthians 3:5–11)

All believers, therefore, must remember the original foundation of the Church and not search for some other foundation. Our hope that the building will always be ordered and stable is based on the certainty that the foundation is Christ. Only in this sense can we say, "*we* are the Church." Only insofar as each of us recognizes that we have been called to the life of grace through the death and resurrection of Christ can this be said. There is no personal merit involved, it is a true vocation which one cannot refuse without losing one's raison d'être, the sense of one's whole existence. Everyone is therefore called to build up the Church, but each one according to the ministry for which he or she has been chosen, without confusion or recrimination or any sense of inferiority. Each person should be happy to play his or her part in the construction of the one temple of God in the complementarity and reciprocity of the whole community and all its members.

There is an ancient text which better allows us to understand the mentality of the Christian community of the first centuries and can also help us reflect on how to build up the Church in our own time. It comes from the work known as *The Shepherd of Hermas*, written between the first and second centuries. The author, whose name we do not know, is known as an "apostolic father" and in some ways resembles one of the "prophets" recognized by the community. He would explain the Scriptures to them in their moments of greatest hardship and give them strength to carry on, bearing witness and spreading the Gospel. In his third vision, the Shepherd of Hermas sees the Church thus:

> The lady took my hand once more, raised me up and made me sit on the bench on the left while she sat down on the right. Raising a splendid rod she said to me: "Do you see something wonderful?" I said: "Lady, I see nothing." She said to me: "Don't you see before you a great tower built on the waters with glittering square stones?"
>
> For the tower was built square by those six young men who had come with her. But myriads of men were carrying stones to it, some dragging them from the depths, others removing them from the land, and they handed them to these six young men. They were taking them and building; and those of the stones that were dragged out of the depths, they placed in the building just as they were: for they were polished and fitted exactly into the other stones, and became so united, one with another, that the lines of joining could not be perceived. And in this way the building of the tower looked as if it were made out of one stone.
>
> Those stones, however, which were taken from the earth suffered a different fate; for the young men rejected some of them, some they fitted into the building, and

> some they cut and cast far away from the tower. Many other stones, however, lay around the tower, and the young men did not use them in building; for some of them were rough, others had cracks in them, others had been made too short, and others were white and round, but did not fit into the building of the tower. Moreover, I saw other stones thrown far away from the tower and falling into the public road; yet they did not remain on the road but were rolled into a pathless place. And I saw others falling into the fire and burning, others falling close to the water, and yet not capable of being rolled into the water, though they wished to be rolled down, and to enter the water.

It is not too difficult for us to grasp the author's idea. He is retelling the parable of the sower (cf. Mt 13:3–9). Here, too, the response to the word of God is dependent on each individual's circumstances in life. By reading on further we can understand the author's vision even more clearly:

> The tower which you see being built is myself, the Church, which appeared to you now and on the former occasion. Ask, then, whatever you like in regard to the tower, and I will reveal it to you. … I asked her, "Why was the tower built upon the waters?" She answered … "It is because our life has been, and will be, saved through water. For the tower was built at the word of the almighty and glorious Name and it is kept together by the invisible power of the Lord."
>
> In reply I said to her, "This is magnificent and marvelous. But who are the six young men who are engaged in building?" And she said, "These are the holy angels of God, who were first created, and to whom the Lord

handed over his whole creation, that they might increase and build up and rule over the whole creation. By these will the building of the tower be finished."

"But who are the other persons who are engaged in carrying the stones?" "These also are holy angels of the Lord, but the former six are more excellent than these. The building of the tower will be finished, and all will rejoice together around the tower, and they will glorify God."... I asked her, "Lady, I should like to know what became of the stones, and what was meant by the various kinds of stones?" In reply she said to me, "Those square white stones which fitted exactly into each other, are apostles, bishops, teachers, and deacons who have lived in godly purity, and have acted as bishops and teachers and deacons chastely and reverently caring for the elect of God. Some of them have fallen asleep, and some still remain alive. And they have always lived in harmony, and been at peace among themselves, and listened to each other. On account of this, they fit perfectly into the building of the tower."

"But who are the stones that were dragged from the depths, and which were laid into the building and fitted in with the rest of the stones previously placed in the tower?" "They are those who suffered for the Lord's sake." "But I wish to know, O Lady, who are the other stones which were carried from the land?" She said, "Those which go into the building without being polished, are those whom God has approved of, for they walked in the straight ways of the Lord and practiced his commandments."

"But who are those who are in the act of being brought and placed in the building?" "They are those who are young in faith and are faithful. But they are admonished by the angels to do good, for no iniquity has been found in them."

"Who then are those whom they rejected and cast away?" "These are the ones who have sinned, and wish to repent. For this reason, they have not been thrown far from the tower, because they will yet be useful in the building, if they repent. Those then who are to repent, if they do repent, will be strong in faith, if they repent while the tower is being built. For if the building be finished, there will be no more room for anyone, and he will be rejected. This privilege, however, will belong only to him who has now been placed near the tower."

"As to those who were cut down and thrown far away from the tower, do you wish to know who they are? They are the sons of iniquity, and they believed in hypocrisy, and wickedness did not depart from them. For this reason, they are not saved, since they cannot be used in the building on account of their iniquities. Therefore, they have been cut off and cast far away on account of the anger of the Lord, for they have roused him to anger. But I shall explain to you the other stones which you saw lying in great numbers, and not going into the building. Those which are rough are those who have known the truth and not remained in it, nor have they been joined to the saints. On this account are they unfit for use."

"Who are those stones that have cracks?" "These are the ones who are at discord in their hearts one with another, and are not at peace among themselves: They indeed keep peace before each other, but when they separate one from the other, wicked thoughts remain in their hearts. These, then, are the cracks which are in the stones. The shortened stones are those who have indeed believed and have the larger share of righteousness; yet they have also a considerable share of iniquity, and therefore they are shortened and not whole." "But who are these, Lady, that are white and round, and yet do not fit into the building of the tower?" She said to me: "These are those who have faith indeed, but they have also the riches of this world. When, therefore, tribulation comes on account of their riches and busyness, they deny the Lord."

I ask her: "Will they be useful for the building?" "When the riches that now seduce them have been circumscribed, then will they be of use to God. For as a round stone cannot become square unless portions be cut off and cast away, so also those who are rich in this world cannot be useful to the Lord unless their riches be cut down. Learn this first from your own case. When you were rich, you were useless; but now you are useful and fit for life. Be useful to God; for you also will be used as one of these stones."

She continued: "The other stones which you saw cast far away from the tower and falling upon the public road and rolling from it into pathless places are those who have indeed believed, but through doubt have abandoned the true path. Thinking, then, that they could find a better way, they wander and become wretched and enter pathless places. Those which fell into the fire and were burned are those who have apostatized forever from the living God … the others which fell near the waters, but could not be rolled into them, these are they who have heard the word, and wish to be baptized in the name of the Lord; but when the purity of the truth comes to their mind, they draw back, and again follow their wicked desires."

The symbolism hidden in this vision of *The Shepherd of Hermas* should provoke in all of us a serious examination of conscience. Basically, we must ask ourselves which kind of stone we are and what kind of image of the temple our Christian life offers to the men and women of our time. Our passing through the Holy Door of the temple of God, which is his Church, therefore, does not take away in the slightest our baptismal responsibility. Rather, it makes us capable of taking on new responsibilities for proclaiming and witnessing to the Gospel.

Here, the words of *The Epistle of Barnabas* come to mind:

> Learn how it will be built in the name of the Lord. ... By obtaining the remission of our sins and hoping in his Name we became new, created afresh. Therefore, God truly dwells within us. How? His word of faith, the call of his promise, the wisdom of his laws, the commandments of his teaching, he himself prophesying in us, he himself dwelling in us, opening for us the door of the temple, which is our mouth, and giving us repentance, all of this leads us out of the bondage of death to the incorruptible temple. For he who desires to be saved looks not to man, but to the One who dwells and speaks in him, being amazed at this, that he has never at any time heard these words from the mouth of the speaker, nor himself ever desired to hear them. This is the spiritual temple built by the Lord. (Chapter 16)

So, the temple of God really does exist. It is present in his Church and made visible by the faithful testimony of those who are not afraid of being isolated and do not shrink away in fear before those who seem to have more sophisticated instruments available to them. We are strong in faith, in charity, and in the hope which empowers us:

You are stones of the temple of the Father, prepared for the building work by God the Father, lifted into place by the cross of Jesus Christ, secured by the cord that is the Holy Spirit. Faith is the lever which lifts you into place, and charity is the road which leads you to God. You are all companions on the journey, bearers of God, bearers of the temple, bearers of Christ and of the Holy Spirit, embellished always by the precepts of Jesus Christ. (Ignatius, *To the Ephesians*, Chapter 9)

7
The Profession of Faith

Passing through the Holy Door, the pilgrim enters St. Peter's Basilica. We have already focused on the significance of this act of entering the basilica. Approaching the Altar of the Confession, and Peter's tomb, Christians are invited to make a profession of faith. The profession of faith is also a sign, and one that is important to understand in all its theological depth because of the value it has for the life of Christians.

The Creed — symbol of faith

An interesting text, written by Rufinus in the fourth century, is a good introduction to the topic of the profession of faith. The book, *A Commentary on the Apostles' Creed*, dedicates a few pages to the origins of the symbol of faith:

> After the ascension of the Lord, when, with the coming of the Holy Spirit, tongues of fire appeared over each of the apostles so that they could speak in different and various languages, so that no foreign people, no

> barbarian language seemed inaccessible to them, they were commanded to set out to each individual nation to preach the word of God. Just as they are leaving and separating from each other, they established in common the norm of their future preaching, so that, although distant from each other, they would not communicate something different to those whom they would invite to embrace the faith of Christ. Therefore, being all together and filled with the Holy Spirit, putting together what each one felt, they composed — as we have said — this brief outline of their future preaching, and decided to give this norm to those who would believe.

They wanted to call it a "symbol" for many good reasons. In fact, in Greek the word *symbol* means "clue," and also "collective contribution" — that is, something which several people put together. In fact, this is precisely what the apostles did in these discourses, putting together what everyone felt. Therefore, they established this sign, in order that people might recognize the one who truly proclaimed Christ, according to the apostolic norms.

Rufinus is not satisfied with simply describing the origins of the symbol [or creed]. In his account, which, it must be said, does not always correspond to the facts, he does remind us of an important truth — namely, that the profession of faith has a normative character in the life of the believing community. It is no coincidence, in fact, that from the fourth century on, this symbol was used as a means of proving one's membership of the different churches, in the unity and truth of the apostolic faith, without any addition or tampering with its contents. The symbol of faith, therefore, since its earliest origins, shows the unity of the Church and the existence of a fundamental text which the baptized can consult to be sure of the beliefs to which they give their assent.

Rufinus also reports another important detail. He states that the profession of faith was made by Christians *publicly*, before the whole community, to express the faith of the entire people of God:

> I believe it is not out of place to recall that in various churches we can find cases of additions being made to these words. However, this is not known to have happened in the Church of Rome, because no heresy originated there, and the ancient form is preserved there. Those who are about to receive baptism repeat the symbol publicly — that is, while the faithful listen — and certainly those who preceded them in faith and now listen would not tolerate the addition of a single word.

This tradition is confirmed in the *Confessions* of Saint Augustine. Here he narrates the conversion of the great scholar Victorinus, as told to him by Simplicianus, described in the *Confessions* as the father of Saint Ambrose. The distinguished philosopher Victorinus liked to read the holy Scriptures and confided in Simplicianus that he agreed with them, and therefore considered himself to be a Christian. Simplicianus responded: "I don't believe you, and I won't count you among the Christian people if I don't see you in the Church of Christ."

Later, Victorinus comes to understand that his adherence to Christ must be expressed by a public profession of faith. The scene described in the *Confessions* is revealing:

> Eventually the time came for him to make his profession of faith. Custom decrees that in Rome those who are approaching your grace in baptism make their profession, standing on a raised platform and using a set form of words which has been entrusted to them and commit-

> ted to memory.
>
> Simplicianus told me that Victorinus had been offered by the priests the option of making his profession of faith privately, for it was customary to offer this concession to people who were likely to lose their nerve through shyness, but that he had chosen rather to proclaim his salvation before the holy company, and that salvation was not the mere rhetoric that he taught, though he had professed that publicly enough. … As he climbed up to make his profession of faith, they all whispered his name to one another in a clamorous outburst of thanksgiving — everyone who knew him, that is, and was there anyone present who did not know him? Then in more subdued tones the word passed from joyful mouth to joyful mouth among them all: "Victorinus, Victorinus!" Spontaneous was their shout of delight as they saw him, and spontaneous their attentive silence to hear him. With admirable conviction he recited the formula of the true faith, and all the people longed to clasp him tenderly to their hearts. (Chapter VIII, 2)

This short extract from the *Confessions* provides us not only with an important insight into the tradition of the profession of faith, but also reveals to us the faith-filled emotion of the believers who heard it. One cannot fail to be moved by these stories. For they belong to a wider tradition that has expressed the faith through simple gestures. Starting from this experience of public recitation of the Creed, which the Church of the first centuries subsequently made explicit, it is possible to delve deeper into the significance of the profession of faith and understand its value in the daily life of the baptized.

The profession of faith, whether it be called the "creed" or "symbol," is a sign of adherence on the part of the baptized to the central content of their faith. The term basically means the summary of the main truths of the Christian faith, accepted by a believer on his baptismal day and shared by him with the entire Christian community for the rest of his life.

A text by Saint Cyril explains the reason for this:

> The symbol of faith was not composed by human opinions, but consists in the collection of the salient points, chosen from all of Sacred Scripture, so as to create a complete doctrine of the faith. And just as the mustard seed contains many branches in a grain, so this compendium of faith contains within it all the knowledge contained in the Old and New Testaments. (*The Catechetical Lectures*, V, 12)

Indeed, in the Bible we can identify some short professions of faith. The Old Testament, although it does not, strictly speaking, contain a profession of faith, preserves a very ancient trace of it which was repeated in the rite of the Passover celebration:

> In the future when your son asks you, "What is the meaning of the decrees and statutes and ordinances that the LORD, our God, has commanded of you," you are to tell your son, "We were slaves to Pharaoh in Egypt, but the LORD brought us out of Egypt with a mighty hand. The LORD performed signs and wonders in our sight, great and terrible things, that he imposed upon Egypt and upon Pharaoh and upon all of his household. He brought us out from there so that he might bring us into and give to us the land that he promised to our fathers. The LORD commanded us to observe all of these statutes and to fear the LORD, our God, so that we might always prosper and be kept

alive, even as we are today." (Deuteronomy 6:20–24)

The New Testament is in a sense, born in a profession of faith. Jesus, from the very outset of his preaching, asked the disciples to profess their faith in him as being the one sent by the Father. Indeed, he worked no miracle that was not accompanied by an explicit or implicit act of faith in him. The scene which takes place at Caesarea in Philippi — and which is so important that it appears in the accounts of all four evangelists — in which Jesus asks his disciples who he is, carries their de facto profession of faith in him: "You are the Christ" (Mk 8:29). This short formula of faith is paralleled in other texts: "Jesus is Lord" (1 Cor 12:3), "my Lord and my God" (Jn 20:28), "Jesus is the Son of God" (1 Jn 4:15).

Starting with these simple professions of faith, the Christian community progressively built up a central nucleus of the Faith, adding on various moments from the life of Jesus or truths about him. An example of this can be found in the oldest text of the New Testament which records the oral profession of faith of the early community: "That Christ died for our sins, in accordance with the Scriptures, that he was buried and that he was raised to life on the third day in accordance with the Scriptures, and that he appeared to Cephas" (1 Cor 15:3–5).

Even in the earliest days of the Church we can find traces of the creed. In the *First Apology of Justin Martyr*, written to Emperor Antoninus Pius in the year 155, we can find evidence of a profession of faith: "God the Father and Lord of all things, Christ the Savior, crucified under Pontius Pilate, the Holy Spirit who, through the mouths of the prophets, foretold all that refers to Jesus." Similar expressions can be found in the works of Tertullian which detail that when a person was presented for baptism, they had to renounce Satan and profess the faith by answering three questions about God the Father, Jesus Christ, and the Holy

Spirit. In this text we also find the first mention of the Church (cf. *On Baptism*).

The oldest text on this subject dates back to the year 215 and is attributed to Hippolytus in his *Traditio apostolica* (*Apostolic Tradition*). It describes the rite of baptism as it was celebrated in the Church of Rome. The responses of the catechumens are those which are still used today in the celebration of baptism:

> The one to be baptized goes down into the waters and the one who is baptizing places his hand on the other's head, saying, "Do you believe in God the Father almighty?" and the one to be baptized replies, "I believe." He then baptizes him a first time keeping his hand on his head. Then he says, "Do you believe in Jesus Christ, the Son of God, born by the Holy Spirit of the Virgin Mary, who died and was buried, who rose from the dead on the third day, ascended into heaven, is seated at the right hand of the Father and will come to judge the living and the dead?" And when the one to be baptized says, "I believe," he is baptized a second time. Then the one baptizing speaks again: "Do you believe in the Holy Spirit, the Holy Church, and in the resurrection of the body?" The one being baptized says, "I believe," and thus he is baptized a third time.

"I believe"

In this profession of faith there are three points worth highlighting.

The first concerns the formula of questioning the candidate. The bishop or priest asks the catechumen to express himself before the whole community to be certain that the person is familiar with the contents of the faith which he is about to embrace in baptism. An awareness of the commitments of baptism is significant in the Christian life. For in baptism, the believer receives the very life of God and is admitted and welcomed into the Church. A new journey begins at this point for the baptized person in which he or she must live as a child of the light and as a disciple of Jesus Christ. Repeatedly, the apostle Paul sets out in his letters the ways a Christian is called to witness to his or her baptism. A short summary is found in the Letter to the Ephesians:

> Cease your lying and speak the truth to each other, for we are all members of one another. If you are angry, do not sin. Do not let the sun set on your anger, and do not give the devil an opening. Anyone who has been stealing must no longer do so; rather, let him labor, performing some honest work with his own hands, so that he may have something to share with those in need. Let no foul word ever pass your lips. Say only what is useful for edification, so that your words may benefit your listeners. And do not grieve the Holy Spirit of God who has marked you with his seal for the day of redemption. Remove all forms of bitterness and wrath and anger and shouting and slander, as well as all malice from your lives. Rather, be kind to one another and compassionate, and forgive one another as God has forgiven you in Christ.
>
> Hence, be imitators of God, as beloved children, and walk in love, as Christ loved us and gave himself up for us as a sacrificial offering whose fragrance is pleasing to God. Fornication and impurity of any kind, as well as greed, should not even be mentioned among you. Such talk is not fitting for saints. You should never engage in any obscene or foolish or suggestive conversation. All this is completely out of place. Instead, you should rather be engaged in offering thanks to God. Once you

> were darkness, but now you are light in the Lord. Live as children of light, for light produces all goodness and righteousness and truth. Discern what the Lord finds pleasing. Take no part in the fruitless deeds of darkness, but rather condemn them openly. (4:25—5:1–4, 8–12)

The second thing worth noting is the Trinitarian structure of the content of faith that is professed. As we have seen, the three questions are focused on the three persons of the Trinity, and this is not coincidental. Faith in Jesus Christ is characterized by faith in God the Father, Son, and Holy Spirit. Here we come face-to-face with the radical teaching of the revelation of Jesus Christ. And it throws a new light on previous revelations, so much so that the fathers of Vatican II stated, "The deepest truth about God and the salvation of man shines out for our sake in Christ, who is both the mediator and the fullness of all revelation" (*Dei Verbum*, 2), such that "we now await no further new public revelation before the glorious manifestation of our Lord Jesus Christ" (4).

To profess our faith in the Trinity means, first, placing ourselves before the mystery of God who reveals himself as the beginning and end of all things. He is the *Father* in whom everything has its beginning, who has placed everything in the world as a sign of his unending love. He is the *Son* who takes flesh out of obedience to the love of the Father, and who is obedient to him in all things, even accepting death on a cross for the salvation of humanity. He is the *Holy Spirit* who continues the work started by Christ and brings it to completion in the fullness of time through the work of sanctification of mankind and the whole of creation. Three persons, therefore, but one single divine nature which manifests the unfathomable mystery of Love.

It is in this context of discussing baptism and the profession of faith that St. Gregory Nazianzen, one of the great thinkers of the ancient world (who earned the title "theologian" for the profound nature of his doctrine) spoke to his catechumens:

> First of all, preserve for me this precious deposit for which I live and fight and with which I desire to die. It makes me able to accept every evil and renounce every pleasure. By "deposit" I mean the profession of faith in the Father, in the Son, and in the Holy Spirit. Today I entrust it to you. With it I will soon immerse you in the waters and then raise you up from those waters. I give it to you, this profession of faith, as a companion and guardian for your whole lives ahead. I give you one single Divinity and Power, who is Three in One, and contains the Three in a distinct way. A Divinity without difference of substance or nature, without higher or lower levels. … From three infinities a single connatural infinity. Each one is in himself all of God. … The God of Three persons considered as one. … I have just started to think of the Unity and here I am immersed in the splendor of the Trinity. I start to think of the Trinity and here I am satiated by the Unity." (*Orations*, 40–41)

Professing faith in the Trinity does not simply mean proclaiming the mystery of God. It also means accepting the consequences of this revelation. Professing that God is Trinity means expressing his life of love, which manifests itself in the communion and in the community of the three persons. The God of Jesus Christ is a God of community and a communion of love (*koinonia).* The first consequence of this in the life of the Christian is the realization that all of life must be built on communion, which is the way in which the God he believes in and entrusts himself to exists. The believer, then, can no longer see himself as an isolated individual, but rather as a person in relationship with others. The word *solitude* disappears from the vocabulary of the Christian and the words *communion* and *community* take its place.

The mystery of faith enters so profoundly into the life of the Christian that it leaves a new understanding of who man is, what life is, and how we are to view the world. The person understands himself in terms of relationship, life is defined as a call to love, and the world discovers once more what it had lost — namely, that it exists for the glory of the creator. Therefore, every time that the Christian says, "In the name of the Father and of the Son and of the Holy Spirit," he affirms in these simple words the truth about himself. He is called to welcome this mystery of love which gives full and lasting meaning to his life.

The third point worth noting concerns the catechumen who replies *"I believe"* in the first person. These words are necessary to express that freedom with which one embraces faith. It is certainly true that behind everything there is always the call of God working through grace, but this does not impede, nor could it, the freedom of every person to express themselves as they see fit. God always creates in freedom, and he offers to every creature the possibility of refusing his creator. It is not true that man becomes freer by refusing God. By denying himself that greater possibility of freedom which comes about through participation in the life of God, man limits himself — it is an illusion of exercising his freedom.

"I believe," therefore, is an expression of total freedom supported by the grace of the Spirit which allows man to glimpse a truth that could never be seen with the naked eye alone. The eyes of faith, on the other hand, because they see with the heart and not only with the mind, reach into places which reason alone could never hope to discover — they reach that which is essential. "I believe," therefore, affirms full awareness of both the content and the responsibility of faith that a person hopes to follow by God's grace.

"We believe"

The profession of faith is not limited only to the baptismal setting. From the fourth century onward, a new element was added to the history of the Creed — as a sign of the unity of the entire Church. This came about during a period of Church history which saw a great intellectual richness. The bishops of antiquity were also great theologians and, with the methods available to them, brought about one of the most coherent forms of what we today would call the "inculturation of the faith." The Church Fathers were well versed in the cultures and philosophies of their time but were also faithful to the word of God. This explains why they never fell into any form of syncretism. They understood that culture, by its very nature, is always open to truth, and when it discovers truth, it wants to make it its own, knowing that only in this way can culture itself progress. To overcome the divisions that were present among Christians, who were often confused by erroneous interpretations or extremist readings of the holy Scriptures, the Church Fathers were periodically called together in councils to define the truth of the faith and reassure believers.

Here we cannot fail to mention the first council of our history, that of Nicaea in the year 325. By happy coincidence, 2025 marks the 1700th anniversary of that event. *Spes Non Confundit* makes a direct reference to this anniversary:

> The Council of Nicaea sought to preserve the Church's unity, which was seriously threatened by the denial of the full divinity of Jesus Christ and hence his consubstantiality with the Father. Some three hundred bishops took part, convoked at the behest of the Emperor Constantine; their first meeting took place in the Imperial Palace on May 20, 325. After various debates, by the grace of the Spirit they unanimously approved the Creed that we still recite each Sunday at the celebration of the Eucharist. The council fathers chose to begin that Creed by using for the first time the expression "We believe"

> as a sign that all the churches were in communion and that all Christians professed the same faith. The Council of Nicaea was a milestone in the Church's history. The celebration of its anniversary invites Christians to join in a hymn of praise and thanksgiving to the Blessed Trinity and in particular to Jesus Christ, the Son of God, "consubstantial with the Father," who revealed to us that mystery of love. At the same time, Nicaea represents a summons to all churches and ecclesial communities to persevere on the path to visible unity and in the search for fitting ways to respond fully to the prayer of Jesus "that they may all be one. As you, Father, are in me and I am in you, may they also be in us, so that the world may believe that you have sent me" (Jn 17:21). (17)

In this Creed, the use of the words "we believe" to express the content of faith is extremely interesting. The change from "I believe" to "we believe" takes nothing away from the personal commitment of each baptized person in professing his or her faith. Instead, it makes explicit something that is already present in the form "I believe." To say "we believe" is to affirm that our faith is the very same faith as that of the Church and not just the faith of an individual believer. It is through the Church that one comes to faith and is reborn on the new path of God. Without the Church the baptized person could not say "I believe," because he would not have any content of faith to profess. From the Council of Nicaea onward, the Creed becomes the sign of genuine, authentic, and orthodox faith which is free of all error. And the profession of faith becomes the criterion which allows bishops across the world to recognize each other in the faith of the ages, the faith of the apostles, and to ensure communion among all the churches.

"We believe," therefore, proclaims that the believer is never alone in his faith and duties. The Church is always present, so much so, that if the conscience of a baptized person is not transformed into an "ecclesial conscience" — a conscience formed by the Church — baptism can do very little for that person.

In the climate of subjectivity that reigns today, it has become ever more difficult to understand the importance of this essential aspect of the Christian faith. Having recourse to one's own conscience is the most intimate and sacred action that any person can undertake to understand and judge the good and evil in his or her own actions. The great subjectivity of modern culture inevitably leads Christians to appeal to their own conscience — and rightly so. No one can interfere with this, and in so doing the person places himself or herself before God aware of his or her responsibility for the decision to be taken. The Christian, however, in consulting his or her conscience, is obliged to check the foundations on which that conscience is built and the content with which it is nourished. For conscience is never neutral. It is nourished by content that either enriches or clouds the mind and heart in the choices of daily life. In today's world, in which communications technology impacts so profoundly on people's consciences, this consideration is of no small importance.

What kind of conscience will the believer have if he nourishes himself on everything except the nourishment which the faith really needs — namely, the word of God transmitted in written and oral form, the teaching of the pope and bishops, and the systematic study offered by catechesis? Such a person's judgment will struggle with the truths of the faith. It is likely that such a person will succumb to one of the various cultural offerings on the market without realizing that often these go against the Faith in a radical way. This is especially true for those who play a public role in society. Clergy and lay people sometimes forget that they should not act in a "schizophrenic" way when the content of faith and the laws of the land diverge. Just as it is not licit to obey a man-made law which contrasts with the law of God, so, too, those who act as legislators and call themselves Christian have no right to barter away the truths of the Faith in the name of a generic sense of tolerance. It goes without saying how far from a true Christian conscience such attitudes are. They indicate a false, and indeed erroneous, vision of the Christian faith that overstates the importance of the phrase "I believe" at the expense of "we believe." The "I" has grown out of all proportion and has forgotten that it should be an "ecclesial I." Instead, it is just an "individual I," the expression of a conscience that has been formed by a culture that is alien to the Faith, and in many ways becomes an alternative to the Faith.

The words "we believe" make us stop and remember that Christians should never adapt their views so much that they become indistinguishable from the children of this world: "You belong to this world, but ... not of this world" (Jn 8:23). To ignore this means negating the choice of faith in its genuineness and specificity, transforming it into a kind of cultural surrogate for people who happen to have been born in a Christian country. The faith of the Church comes before the faith of the individual, and the individual cannot set himself up as the arbiter of the Church's faith without losing his way.

Memory versus oblivion

A well-known passage from early Christian literature helps us reflect on that which, always and everywhere, should be the *norm* of Christian living. In the *Epistle to Diognetus* we read:

> Christians do not differ from other men either by territory, nor by the way they speak, nor by the style of their clothes. In fact, they do not live in particular cities, they do not use any strange language, and they do not adopt a special way of life. The doctrine that they follow was not invented by them following the reflection and research

of men who love novelties, nor do they rely, as some do, on a human philosophical system.

They reside in both Greek and barbarian cities, and although they follow the local customs in their way of dressing, in their way of eating, and in the rest of their lives, they propose an admirable but paradoxical way of life. They live in their own homeland but do so as though they were strangers; they fulfill all the duties of citizens but are detached like foreigners; every foreign region is their homeland, yet every homeland is foreign to them. Like all others, they marry and have children, but they do not abandon their children. They share a table, but not a bed.

They live in the flesh, but not according to the flesh. They live on earth but have their citizenship in heaven. They observe the established laws but, in their way of life, they go beyond the laws. They love everyone and are persecuted by everyone. Even if they are not known, they are condemned; they are killed, and they revive. They are poor and make many rich; they lack everything and abound in everything. They are despised and in contempt they find their glory; they are denounced and also proclaimed to be just. They are reviled, and they bless; they are treated outrageously, and reciprocate with honor. When they do good, they are punished as if they were evildoers; when they are punished, they rejoice as if life were given to them. The Jews wage war against them as against foreigners, and the Greeks persecute them; but those who hate them cannot give a reason for their hatred. In short, Christians represent in the world what the soul is in the body. … God has placed them in a place that they are not allowed to abandon." (cf. V, VI)

The *Catechism of the Catholic Church* has a lovely expression which indicates the complementarity and reciprocity of the two forms of profession of faith. It states:

> I believe (*Apostles' Creed*) is the faith of the Church professed personally by each believer, principally during Baptism. We believe (*Niceno-Constantinopolitan Creed*) is the faith of the Church confessed by the bishops assembled in council or more generally by the liturgical assembly of believers. I believe is also the Church, our mother, responding to God by faith as she teaches us to say both I believe and We believe. (167)

In some ways these words echo the message which John gave by constantly underlining the "ecclesial we" of the faith:

> What existed from the beginning, what we have heard, what we have seen with our own eyes, what we have looked at and touched with our hands — we are speaking of the Word of life. That life was made visible; we have seen it and bear witness, proclaiming to you the eternal life that was with the Father and was revealed to us. What we have seen and heard we declare to you so that you may have fellowship with us. For our fellowship is with the Father and with his Son Jesus Christ. We are writing this so that our joy may be complete. (1 John 1:1–4)

Within this constant work of transmitting the Faith, we can understand why various Fathers of the Church wanted believers to learn the words of the creed by rote. Rufinus, whom we have quoted before, says that this command came directly from the apostles: "The Twelve ruled that these norms should not be written on any old sheets of paper, but rather committed to memory because it was certain that no one would have learned them from a written text." The Creed, in other words, was to be written only on the minds and hearts of Christians. In this way it would remain a constant memory of their coming to the Faith and become a hymn of praise to the Father for the benefits of his grace. The words of Saint Augustine are, in this context, highly significant: "The words of the Creed should not be written down so as to memorize them, but they should be committed to memory by listening to them. And don't write them down, either, after having learned them, but rather keep them always in your memory and in this way bring them to mind." In summary, the Christian is called every day to express his loyalty by professing his faith in Christ, which is the faith of the whole Church.

Reflecting on the Creed allows us to identify the dynamics of the Faith. We can see, first of all, that it comes from a conviction that must always be passed on — a transmission which must never stop and which is based on the missionary nature of the Church, tasked by the Lord with bringing the Gospel to the whole world and to every creature (cf. Mt 28:19–20). The Church will never tire of tramping the paths of the earth to share with those who do not yet possess it, this announcement of truth which recalls man to his true identity. Faith is not a vague feeling that we cradle deep inside, nor is it a generic commitment that sometimes emerges because we feel gratified by it. Rather, it is the full, total, and unhesitating response given to Christ who calls us to become his disciples and to be perfect. For this profession of faith, the martyrs gave their lives, showing each of us the great path that every true disciple of Christ must be prepared to follow.

There seems no better way to conclude this chapter than with the words of Saint Ambrose in his treatise on the *Exposition of the Christian Faith*. In fact, they help us understand why, even today, the Christian should constantly refer to the profession of faith and respect the validity of the early Church Fathers' command that it be studied by heart. In all times and all seasons the Creed remains the anchor to which we should cling so that Christians may always remember in whom they are rooted and toward whom they are going: "This creed is a spiritual seal, it is the meditation of our heart and its constant defense: without a doubt it is the treasure we keep in our hearts."

8
Charity

"It is not holy places which save us but holy actions." This expression of Saint Jerome seems the perfect way to start this chapter. No one should think that the practice of pilgrimage and the celebration of the indulgence are some kind of magical formula for obtaining eternal life. It is the life of charity which gives those actions their ultimate meaning and their true efficacy. It is true, Saint Jerome was not a man who loved pilgrimages. Indeed, he tried to avoid them as some of his letters prove unequivocally! His phrase, quoted above, however, says something significant.

In the eighteenth century, Voltaire, a powerful polemicist who was certainly no believer, wrote almost a mirror image of the words of Jerome:

> I admire the fact that religion does not consist only of opinions about intelligible metaphysics or in various structures, but rests rather in adoration and in justice. Doing good — this is its worship. Being under the power of God — this is its doctrine. If the Muslim cries

> out: "Woe be to you if you do not make a pilgrimage to Mecca," and the priest warns: "Woe betide you if you do not go to the Madonna of Loreto," true religion laughs at both Mecca and Loreto but defends the oppressed and comes to the aid of the poor. (Voltaire, "Theism," in *Dizionario filosofico*, Milan, 2013)

We should not absolutize this quote of course, but it does represent an attitude often held by our contemporaries. People admire works of charity much more than the practice of pilgrimage, especially when pilgrimage loses its specifically religious meaning. Besides, charity is the preeminent sign of the Christian faith and is the way it manifests its own credibility. In the context of the Jubilee, we cannot forget the invitation of the apostle Peter: "Above all, maintain the fervor of your love for one another, because love covers a multitude of sins" (1 Pt 4:8).

Charity, then, has a particular place in the life of faith and can be seen as a significant expression of conversion. That is why, as was outlined in chapter 2, Pope Francis included it in the bull of indiction for the Holy Year, *Spes Non Confundit* (cf. nos. 7–15) as one of the signs of hope.

Toward a fuller understanding of charity

We must be very clear that, for the Christian, there is no such thing as love without faith. Love, when illuminated by faith, reveals the true meaning of Christian love as a pure giving of self without asking for anything in return. To better understand Christian charity, therefore, we must look to revelation and allow it to enlighten and illuminate our way of thinking, to grasp the characteristics which love possesses.

In the Christian faith, love is not a word we should use lightly, without realizing the power which it contains, because this little word expresses the very nature of God himself. Among the many expressions used in the New Testament to say "God," the one which has greatest impact is used only once, in the First Letter of John: "God is love" (4:8). Here, in this simple phrase, we find the definitive content of the Christian faith and can see what makes it different from the other religions of the world.

Yet even in this simple expression, certain conditions are added to the basic understanding of love that man already possesses, which could not have come from him alone, and which he cannot fully understand. Because by affirming that God is love we also recognize the *way* in which God loves. He loves by giving all of himself without ever asking for anything back. His love is expressed fully when the innocent one offers his life for the salvation of all humanity — a humanity which still languishes in sin and, therefore, in the refusal of God. This explains why the Easter mystery is the true center of the Christian faith, because it reveals to us the Trinitarian mystery of a God who participates fully and actively in the history of humanity.

A quick glance at the teachings of the apostles John and Paul can help deepen our understanding of Christian love. An important point to note from the writings of John is that, unlike the authors of the Synoptic Gospels, he never uses the word *conversion*, not even in reference to the need for belief. It is certainly true that the concept is implicit in his Gospel, but his basic idea is crystal clear: When one becomes a disciple of the Lord, one is called to abandon everything and follow the Master.

It is possible to follow Jesus, only if the person loves and has faith in his saving words. In other words, at the outset of love, there is a profound faith in the word of the Lord. But only by acting on it do we truly arrive at love. Therefore, for John, love for our neighbor becomes a new commandment given by the Master, and it is in observing this commandment that Jesus' true disciples will be recognized.

These initial points make clear that no one can be a believer if they do not love and, vice versa, they cannot say they love if they do not also believe. Believing and loving, therefore, are the two requirements of the Christian life which sum up all the others. They are indispensable requirements for anyone who wants to be a disciple of Christ. A person cannot truly be said to have faith if that faith does not grow and evolve into love. But, similarly, a person cannot truly possess love if that love does not begin in faith — a faith which recognized the never-before-seen face of the Master as presented by the Church. As Pope Francis writes in his first encyclical *Lumen fidei*: "God can give no greater guarantee of his love, as Saint Paul reminds us (cf. Rom 8:31–39). Christian faith is thus faith in a perfect love, in its decisive power, in its ability to transform the world and to illuminate time. 'We know and believe the love that God has for us' (1 Jn 4:16). In the love of God revealed in Jesus, faith perceives the foundation on which all reality and its final destiny rest" (15).

Continuing with Saint John's reflections on love, we come across another interesting point. Toward the end of his Gospel, in the section known as the farewell discourses, there is a highly significant detail. Chapter 14 is particularly revealing. In the first part, John speaks of the necessity of faith as a means of overcoming difficulties which the disciples will encounter and as a means of guaranteeing that the Father will listen to their requests (vv. 1–14). But from verse 15 onward, and throughout the rest of the discourse, the noun *faith* and the verb *to believe* are replaced by the noun *love* and the verb *to love*.

It is as though he is saying that union with the Lord, which faith allows to happen, must come about through love, which is the high point and the most sublime expression of the life of communion with Christ. The use of the word *remain*, which has a special significance in the Gospel of John, and which starts to be used ever more frequently after chapter 15, confirms this idea. The follower of the Lord lives in a loving relationship which is permanent, and which manifests itself in the love of the believer.

There can be no mistake, however, when it comes to establishing how we are to arrive at this love. It comes about through a progressive advancement in faith, which is achieved through a constant abandoning of oneself into the hands of the Father. If the Christian is able to arrive at this point of total love, though, it is only because God made the first move. It is God who generates this new life by calling a person to salvation. So, when one comes to faith, and is called to participate in the divine life, one must grow in love to complete the work which has been started.

In the same way, the evangelist teaches us that growth in the Christian life is possible only if we get to know the Son of God and his revelation ever more deeply. This knowledge, far from being something theoretical, involves knowing his voice (cf. 1 Jn 4:4–8) and, therefore, recognizing him. So, if God is love, those who are born from him will have the same characteristics (1 Jn 3:9). They will be motivated by love, not in a secondary way, but by their very nature. Only if we welcome the person of the Son and love him, believing in his word, will we be able to understand what Jesus says: "For the Father himself loves you because you have loved me and have come to believe that I came from God" (Jn 16:27). In these words, more than anywhere else, we can see faith united to love. A love which requires a profession of faith in the person of the Son, and requires, too, the abandoning of self, so as to be one with Christ. In a way, what is being said here is that the truth of our life flows from the love which recognizes in Jesus the one sent by God (Jn 8:32; 12:40) and allows us to place our trust in him.

Finally, it is no coincidence that the Gospel of John, when describing the scene on Calvary, places close to the cross the "disciple whom [Jesus] loved" (Jn 19:26). The other disciples certainly believed, but they fled when faced with the impossibility of fully understanding the significance of Jesus' death. But this was not the case for John. He was able to stay in that place from which the intellect flees and where all human endeavor seems to come up short (cf. Lk 24:21).

So, while all the other disciples return, disappointed, to the work they had been doing before following Jesus (cf. Jn 21:2), John remains strong and faithfully perseveres, even though, humanly, he seems to be acting against reason. But it is precisely because of this perseverance in faith that John turns out to be the only one able to recognize the Master. Even when the Lord hides himself or disguises himself in such a way that the others cannot recognize him, John does recognize him and says, "It is the Lord" (Jn 21:7). No one else can do this because no one else has the strength of love which can go beyond appearances to arrive at the essential. We can understand, then, why the Risen One said to Peter, "If it should be my will that he remain until I come, how does that concern you?" (Jn 21:22). Thus, "the saying then spread among the brethren that this disciple would not die" (v. 23). Love will never die. It will remain "to the end" because the sun of love never sets.

A brief glance at the letters of Paul confirms the teaching of John and adds further insights. For Paul, love holds a primacy that can never be matched by anything else or by any person. That is why he can write rhetorically, "If God is for us, who can be against us?" (Rom 8:31), and, in the same chapter, shortly afterward, "neither death, nor life, nor angels, nor principalities, nor present things, nor things to come, nor powers, nor height, nor depth, nor any other creature will be able to separate us from the love of God" (vv. 38–39). It is because of this, Paul reminds us, that as believers we are more than victors, so much so that we need not fear even death, the final enemy. The certainty of this victory however depends only on the fact that we have been loved by God (cf. v. 37). We are so deeply united to this love that our whole personal existence — not only that of believers —

takes place within the context of this love.

"If I ... do not have love, I am nothing" (1 Cor 13:2). This sums up perfectly the understanding of Paul and fits perfectly with the affirmation of John: "Whoever does not abide in me will be thrown away like a withered branch" (Jn 15:6). Or, to put it more directly, "Whoever does not love remains in death" (1 Jn 3:14). The expression "I am nothing" perhaps does not make a huge impact in modern English, but in the way it is used by the apostle it expresses a profound and overwhelming truth. Love, according to Paul, is the essence of the person, and each person is fully realized only and exclusively insofar as he or she loves.

But we must take care here. We are not talking about a love which comes from deep within us, rather we are talking about the love that has been placed in us by God. Before being able to love, every person must be loved by God. It is only in these circumstances that love can be authentic, genuine, and effective. Thus we can understand the apostle in the Letter to the Ephesians when he says, "because he had such great love for us" (Eph 2:4). This expression demonstrates the originality of the Christian faith and protects it from any possible misunderstanding. Indeed, if we do not understand it in this way, we can easily fall into contradictions, and it becomes impossible to truly understand ourselves.

It is the letter to the Corinthians quoted earlier which leads us to make these observations. One grammatical detail in the letter makes this especially clear. The love (*agape*) of which Paul speaks is written without a definite article. This grammatical detail allows us to interpret it in an absolute sense. In this case, therefore, *agape* can indicate only Jesus Christ. Without him and without the knowledge we must have of him — the apostle seems to say — everything the believer might achieve would make no sense and have little effect. Even the highest testimony of faith — namely, martyrdom — would become meaningless and useless. "If I give away everything to feed the poor and hand over my body to be burned, but do not have love, I achieve nothing" (1 Cor 13:3).

Only in Christ, then, does the love of the Father become visible and perceptible in a historical sense. God shows his love by the fact that, while we were still sinners, Christ died for us. The primacy of the love of God and its gratuitousness are both the font and the origin of every decision made by human beings to live for him. It is in this sense that the idea put forward by Paul in his Letter to the Galatians can be best understood: "All that matters is faith expressing itself through love" (Gal 5:6). Put another way, love renders faith effective and allows it to become the active ingredient of that freedom about which the apostle speaks throughout his letter. Paul, too, believes that faith and love constitute the identity of the Christian. Love is what generates perfection (cf. Col 3:14), and faith is what allows love to truly be itself.

Finally, love has a spiritual dimension. It "has been poured into our hearts through the Holy Spirit that has been given to us" (Rom 5:5). Or to put it even more simply, the apostle refers to the love which comes from the Spirit (cf. Rom 15:30). The action of the Spirit is a guarantee of unity because both faith and love come from the same origin. By seeing love as the natural action of the Spirit, Paul rediscovers the Trinitarian perspective of the content of faith and, at the same time, shows its premise, its foundation, and its certainty. The content of faith, then, is love, which reveals itself and asks to be welcomed and not refused, so as to give all of us the ultimate sense of our existence.

The meaning of love

> What good is it, my brethren, if someone claims to have faith but does not have good works? Can such faith save

> him? Suppose a brother or sister is naked and lacks his or her daily food. If one of you says to such a person, "Go in peace; keep warm and eat well," but does not take care of that person's physical needs, what is the good of that? In the same way, faith by itself is dead if it does not have works. But perhaps someone will say, "You have faith and I have works." Show me your faith without works, and by works I will show you my faith. (James 2:14–18)

This passage from the letter written by the apostle James cannot fail to stir us even today. It is a text which leaves no room for compromise. But Christian charity should not be subject to compromise. Along with faith and truth it constitutes the ultimate motivation for a believer's actions.

The *love principle* will always be the most coherent form of Christian revelation in the life of the Church. Love forces each of us to go the extra mile. In love, we perceive the gratuitousness that is required for faith to understand itself in the light of grace and God's intervention in our lives. In love, we also understand what it means for man to entrust himself completely, intellect and will, to the God who reveals himself. Without this context, faith risks being reduced to a kind of vague feeling and its study to a mere metaphysical theory.

Acting with love, however, does not mean setting aside knowledge and study, or acting against reason. *Au contraire.* Love is the highest form of knowledge because it allows us to go beyond ourselves and meet others, reaching the depths of their being and instilling in them the same desire for love. Love forces us to think, but, of course, not everything can be understood solely in the context of reason. The great philosopher Blaise Pascal successfully summarized this idea: "The heart has its reasons which reason does not know." There are reasons, therefore, which are specific to the heart, and no one can avoid them without running the risk of being unable to truly love.

Love "knows" a person in a very particular way: by entering into communion with the person and always seeking their good. In this way, every person feels welcomed and understood for who they are, without judgment, knowing they are loved just for being themselves. The great Doctor of the Church Saint Bonaventure praised this path and recommended it as one to follow, when he wrote: "When faith gives its assent, not driven by reason, but by the love one has for Christ, then it also desires reason."

Christians have a duty to be the voice of the poor. Our *speaking out* is a concrete testimony that, first and foremost, recognizes and reaches out to those who are victims of poverty. Poverty is an enemy which is the constant companion of so many people in their daily lives. Indeed, it seems inexplicable that the number of poor people continues to multiply in a society which gets richer every day.

There is a serious danger we may encounter on the path toward the Jubilee. That danger is skepticism about our ability to solve problems caused by the poverty we see around us. Being unable to resolve these problems can lead to feelings of indifference or negativity. But there is a different path we can follow. Starting in our own small way, even if it seems like just a drop in the ocean, we can try to help those around us who are deprived of the means to live in a dignified way.

Charity knows no bounds, and it does not allow us to stop and rest along the way. We must do all we can for everyone who needs it. Recognizing our neighbor should not be based on our feelings but should be a genuine response to those who are in need and experiencing poverty. Jesus' famous parable of the good Samaritan, which tells of the man attacked by robbers while traveling from Jerusalem to Jericho, teaches us this. We cannot pass by those in need, deciding for ourselves what kind of help to dispense. Rather, when we see an immediate and urgent need, and witness the reality of the person asking for assistance, it is then that we recognize our neighbor.

Only by leaving behind our egoism are we able to love and to recognize how to love. Otherwise, we will remain imprisoned by doubt and never know the certainty of love. When can I ever be certain that I have loved? When will my love truly be selfless and not conditioned by the desire to be loved in return? These questions can only be answered when we open ourselves fully to love's mystery and do not prevent love entering deep within us and transforming us. It is not an easy path, but it is the only one we can take if we want to be certain of loving.

The words of the Shepherd of Hermas can help us answer these questions:

> Take a stone and throw it up to the sky and see if you can touch it. Or again, take a squirt of water, and squirt it up to heaven — see if you can bore through it. I reply: "Sir, how can these things be? For both these things are beyond our power." Now consider the power which comes from above. The hailstone is a very small drop, and yet, when it falls on a man's head, what pain it causes! Or again, take a drop which falls on the ground from the tiles, and bores through the stone. Think then ... the smallest things falling from above on the earth have great power. So likewise, the divine Spirit coming from above is powerful.

Looking ahead to the next Jubilee, each of us should hear (as though addressed to ourselves) the words which, in the second century, the Bishop of Rome, Pope Clement, addressed to the Christians in Corinth:

> Let he who has the charity of Christ follow his com-

mandments. Who can describe the [blessed] bond of the love of God? What man is able to tell the excellence of its beauty, as it ought to be told? The height to which love exalts is unspeakable. Love unites us to God. Love covers a multitude of sins. Love bears all things, is long-suffering in all things. There is nothing base, nothing arrogant in love. Love admits of no schisms; love gives rise to no seditions; love does all things in harmony. By love have all the elect of God been made perfect; without love nothing is well-pleasing to God. In love has the Lord taken us to himself. On account of the love he bore us, Jesus Christ our Lord gave his blood for us by the will of God; his flesh for our flesh, and his soul for our souls. You see, beloved, how great, and wonderful a thing is love, and that there is no declaring its perfection? Who is fit to be found in it, except those that God has made worthy? Let us pray, therefore, and implore of his mercy, that we may live blameless in love, free from all human partialities for one above another. All the generations from Adam even unto this day have passed away; but those who, through the grace of God, have been made perfect in love, now possess a place among the godly, and it shall be made manifest at the revelation of the kingdom of Christ. … Blessed are we, beloved, if we keep the commandments of God in the harmony of love; that so through love our sins may be forgiven us. (*Letter to the Corinthians*, 49–50)

9
The Return

The ultimate end point of the Jubilee pilgrimage is not the Holy Door, but the return home to everyday life. This should not surprise us, but rather help us to see the real meaning of setting out on pilgrimage to celebrate the Holy Year. Of course, the year itself is a special event, in many senses a unique one. The fact that it is celebrated only once every twenty-five years is a reminder of the exceptional nature of the Jubilee and its capacity to help Christians benefit from the graces offered them. But its real aim is something else. That aim can be summarized as strengthening the pilgrims' faith and reinvigorating their role as witnesses and evangelizers.

Faith and witness require constancy, otherwise everything becomes temporary and affected by passing moods rather than constant effort. The effort of having made the pilgrimage, and the joy of having lived an experience of faith, will shape our everyday life, and it is there, day after day, that we must bear powerful witness to a faith whose sun never sets.

The most obvious thing which the pilgrim will bring home

will surely be the experience of praying in holy places. Visiting Rome will have helped the pilgrim see that his or her faith is shared by many other believers, given that millions of pilgrims are expected in the city of Peter and Paul for the Jubilee. This too is an expression of faith which deserves to be witnessed at a time when popular culture bombards us with images far from ideal for communicating the content of the Faith. This experience of belonging will help people understand that the Church of Christ is something bigger than their daily practice and is in fact the foundation of their experience in the local church. For the Church of Christ is always present where the Spirit of the risen Lord is present, as it is he who leads us to the definitive meeting with the Father.

When, in the profession of faith, pilgrims recite: "I believe in one, holy, catholic, and apostolic Church," the memory of the Jubilee in Rome will give a deeper meaning to this formula. People will discover in these words a Church which has no boundaries of language, race, people, or nation. A communion of persons who love one another and bear witness to that love through a sacramental life which makes them ever more holy, despite the difficulties of everyday life. The Church is thus seen as a house we never finish building, entrusted to Peter, to the Twelve and their successors, so that they may always confirm the brethren in the faith. The Church is a profound unity that no one is permitted to damage or break.

The words of the saintly Bishop Cyprian should sound as a warning against distancing ourselves from the Church or doubting its holiness and credibility:

> We should all firmly believe in and maintain this unity, but especially those of us who are bishops, so that we may prove the episcopate to be one and undivided. Let no one deceive the brothers by false teaching; let no one dam-

age the truth of the faith with perfidious machinations. … The Church is also one, though spread far and wide by its ever-increasing fruitfulness. There are many rays of the sun, but one light. There are many branches of a tree, but one strength from its mighty root. From one spring flow many streams, and though they are multiplied in rich abundance, yet they are still united in one source. You cannot separate a ray of light from the sun because its unity does not allow division. You can break a branch from a tree, but when broken, it will not be able to bud. Cut a stream off from its source and it dries up. It is the same with the Church. Filled with the light of the Lord, it shines its rays over the whole world, yet everywhere it is one and the same light that shines, and the body is not divided. The Church's fruitfulness spreads branches over the whole world. It sends forth her rivers, freely flowing, yet the source is one, and she is one mother, plentiful in fruitfulness. We are born from her womb, nourished by her milk, given life by her spirit. …

This sacrament of unity, this unbreakable bond of concord, is demonstrated in the Gospel, when the coat of the Lord Jesus Christ is not at all divided nor cut, but is received as a whole garment by those who cast lots for it. Scripture says, "Because the coat was seamless, woven in one piece from top to bottom, they said, 'Let us not tear it, but cast lots for it'" [Jn 21:23–24]. That coat had a unity from the top down — that is, unity that came from heaven and the Father — that could not be torn by those who received and possessed it. It is whole and undivided. No one who splits and divides the Church of Christ can possess the garment of Christ. (*Unity of the Catholic Church*)

Our return home should also be a moment to rediscover the importance of silent prayer in the depths of our being, alone with the Father who is in heaven and who sees everything in our hearts (cf. Mt 6:5–6). The beautiful prayer with which Saint Anselm began writing one of his works (the *Proslogion*) comes to mind, and it is a prayer which everyone can make their own:

> Enter deep into your mind, send away everything except God, send away everything which does not help you in searching for him. And, after having closed the door, search for him. Lord, teach my heart where and how to search for you, where and how to find you. Lord if you are not here where will I search for you in your absence? If, though, you are everywhere, why do I not see you here present? Of course, you live in an inaccessible light. Who will lead me to that light so that I can see you? And by what signs and in what form will I recognize you? Teach me to search for you, and show yourself to the one who seeks you, for I cannot search you out, if you do not show me how, and I cannot find you if you do not show yourself to me. Let me search for you by desiring you, let me desire you by searching for you, let me find you by loving you, and let me love you by finding you. … For I do not ask to understand so that I may believe, but I ask to believe so that I might understand. For I believe this too … if I do not believe I will not understand.
>
> These words find an echo in the Imitation of Christ: "Close the door behind you and call Jesus, your beloved, to yourself. Stay with him in your cell, because nowhere else will you find such peace." (Book 1)

It is from this base that the awareness of finding Christ ever present, *really present* in the Eucharist, should grow. Here we find the true mystery of faith, which remains unchanged, a permanent sign of a pilgrimage which will end only when the Lord comes. The Eucharist means that Jesus is always present on the altar, truly present in his risen body, a pledge for our lives. No special technique is required to access this mystery. We modern mystics of the 21st century are given the same chance that was given to people in the past: to contemplate Christ face-to-face, to see the face of God, and to be still in the silence and in the lasting joy of being with Jesus, asking for nothing, repeating like Peter, that "it is good for us to be here" (Mt 17:4).

Finally, on the Lord's Day the pilgrim will understand how beautiful and joyful it is that brothers and sisters come together. Each Sunday should be lived as a moment of resurrection that celebrates Christ and encourages the hope that we will share his destiny by participating in the life of the Church. These points are made very clearly, respecting the circumstances of our time, in the apostolic letter which John Paul II wrote on the meaning of Sundays, *Dies Domini*:

> Sunday appears as the supreme day of faith. It is the day when, by the power of the Holy Spirit, who is the Church's living "memory" (cf. Jn 14:26), the first appearance of the risen Lord becomes an event renewed in the "today" of each of Christ's disciples. Gathered in his presence in the Sunday assembly, believers sense themselves called like the apostle Thomas: "Put your finger here, and see my hands. Put out your hand, and place it in my side. Doubt no longer, but believe" (Jn 20:27). Yes, Sunday is the day of faith. This is stressed by the fact that the Sunday Eucharistic liturgy, like the liturgy of other solemnities, includes the Profession of Faith. Recited or sung, the Creed declares the baptismal and Paschal character of Sunday, making it the day on which in a special way the baptized

> renew their adherence to Christ and his Gospel in a rekindled awareness of their baptismal promises. Listening to the word and receiving the Body of the Lord, the baptized contemplate the risen Jesus present in the "holy signs" and confess with the apostle Thomas: "My Lord and my God!" (Jn 20:28). (29)

The Jubilee pilgrimage, therefore, will not have taken us away from the life we lead every day, but will have strengthened that life by inserting it into the mystery of grace which will have been lived in an extraordinary way during the Holy Year. Our faith will grow in the knowledge that each day we are called to follow Christ and allow ourselves to be guided only by him. And Christ is never far away from us. He is deep in our hearts, allowing us to live always in his presence. Knowing that we are in the presence of the Lord is the reminder we need to differentiate between the essential and the ephemeral, and to recognize how we truly ought to live, despite a thousand ideas to the contrary.

At the end of the Jubilee pilgrimage our faith will have been revived by the hope that we have experienced, thus allowing us to look to the future with a different perspective. Faith in the promise of Jesus that, where he is, we will be too, because he has gone to prepare a place for us (cf. Jn 14:2–3), should remain in the mind and the heart of the pilgrim as the real fruit of the Jubilee celebrations. To grow in hope, without allowing anyone or anything to rob us of that hope, whatever may happen in life, means becoming witnesses of his presence. The conclusion of *Spes Non Confundit* can and should be understood as an invitation addressed to every pilgrim:

> May it help us to recover the confident trust that we require, in the Church and in society, in our interpersonal relationships, in international relations, and in

> our task of promoting the dignity of all persons and respect for God's gift of creation. May the witness of believers be for our world a leaven of authentic hope, a harbinger of new heavens and a new earth (cf. 2 Pt 3:13), where men and women will dwell in justice and harmony, in joyful expectation of the fulfillment of the Lord's promises. Let us even now be drawn to this hope! Through our witness, may hope spread to all those who anxiously seek it. (25)

And so, the journey continues. The thought of reaching the Holy Door to celebrate the Jubilee quickens the pace of every pilgrim, filling him or her with a missionary vigor that will continue every day without weakening. This is what commitment to the New Evangelization is all about, and it needs, first and foremost, Christians who are capable of conversion and conviction.

We have two thousand years of history behind us. But the future which lies ahead knows no bounds. Our gaze is fixed on that future. It belongs to all of us, but in a special way it belongs to the young who, by their very nature, are full of hope and always able to dream. The future always belongs to them. And for the believer, the future is not something vague. We know where we are going, and we know who awaits us. The certainty of Christian hope offers us this clear perspective. In all circumstances it is for us to establish the presence of Christ and his Church in the years to come. The question posed by Jesus, "When the Son of Man comes, will he find faith on the earth?" (Lk 18:8) is not a rhetorical one, and it cannot remain unanswered.

The faith lives by being transmitted. We are all responsible and involved in this process, so that always and everywhere the faith which has been passed to us might be transmitted coherently to future generations. Only in this way will the future be full of meaning, because once more it will be set on the path of salvation revealed by Christ, the one savior of the world, yesterday, today, and forever.

In preparation for the Jubilee Year 2025, the Exploring Prayer series delves into the various dimensions of prayer in the Christian life. These brief, accessible books can help you learn to dialogue with God and rediscover the beauty of trusting in the Lord with humility and joy.

Prayer Today: A Challenge to Overcome
Notes on Prayer: Volume 1
by Angelo Comastri
In order to have saints, what is needed are people of authentic prayer, and authentic prayer is that which inflames with a fire of love. Only in this way is it possible to lift the world and bring it near to the heart of God. To pray in truth, we must present ourselves before God with the open wounds of our smallness and our sin. Only in this way will the encounter with God be an encounter of liberation and redemption.

Praying with the Psalms
Notes on Prayer: Volume 2
by Gianfranco Ravasi
This little guide to the Psalms includes four cardinal points: a general reflection on prayer, the breath of the soul; a panoramic look at the psalmic texts; a portrait of the two protagonists, God and the worshipper, but also the intrusion of the presence of evil; and final-

ly, an anthology of brief commentaries on the Psalms most dear to tradition and the liturgy. The hope is that all the faithful may draw fully from this wonderful treasury of prayers.

The Jesus Prayer
Notes on Prayer: Volume 3
by Juan Lopez Vergara
This book explores the unique experience of the fatherhood of God for Jesus Christ, whom he calls Abba — which in his native Aramaic language means "Dad." Throughout his earthly life, Jesus is in contact dialogue with Abba. From his Baptism in the Jordan through his public ministry and ultimately his crucifixion, this relationship will mark him forever, transforming his life, and our lives, too.

Praying with Saints and Sinners
Notes on Prayer: Volume 4
by Paul Brendan Murray
The saints whose writings on prayer and meditation are explored in this book are among the most celebrated in the great spiritual tradition. The aim of this book is to discover what help the great saints can offer those of us who desire to make progress in the life of prayer, but who find ourselves being constantly deflected from our purpose, our tentative efforts undermined perhaps most of all by human weakness.

Parables on Prayer
Notes on Prayer: Volume 5
by Anthony Pitta
What characterizes, in a singular way, Jesus's teaching on prayer is the recourse to parables. Jesus did not invent a new system for praying. Jesus was not a hermit, a Buddhist monk, or a yogi. He instead chose the daily life of his people to teach prayer with parables. This book explores the parables in the Gospels explicitly related to prayer. The reader is guided by Jesus, the original teacher of prayer with parables.

The Church in Prayer
Notes on Prayer: Volume 6
by Carthusian Monks
Carthusian Monks reside in several international monasteries. Founded in 1084 by Saint Bruno, the Order of Carthusians are dedicated to prayer, in silence, in community. Like other cloistered religious, the Carthusians live a life focused on prayer and contemplation.

The Prayer of Mary and the Saints
Notes on Prayer: Volume 7
by Catherine Aubin
When Mary appears, anywhere in the whole world, the places where she appears have points in common with the biblical places where she stayed and lived. This book reviews these places, examining what they reveal to us about Mary's identity, and what the inner spaces are that Mary asks us to dwell in today. This book also explores the unique relationship two holy women each had with Mary, leading us toward a new, deep revelation of Mary's closeness to each of us.

The Prayer Jesus Taught Us: The "Our Father"
Notes on Prayer: Volume 8
by Hugh Vanni
This book identifies the theological-biblical structure underlying the Lord's Prayer and situates it in the living environment of the early Church. This will give us a framework of reference, and as a result we will see first the antecedents in Mark, then the systematic presentation of Matthew, Paul's push forward, the accentuation of Luke, and, finally, the mature synthesis found in John.